It Makes Me Want To Praise When I Remember God's Faithfulness

Volume 2

Susan Stem

It Makes Me Want To Praise When I Remember God's Faithfulness.

Cover Design by Ruth E. Griffin/Studio Griffin

Cover Illustration by © Jimmy Brown

Photos used by author with permission.

First Edition

ISBN-13: 978-1-954818-62-0

Library of Congress Control Number: 2026912272

1 2 3 4 5 6 7 8 9 10

DEDICATION

This volume is first and foremost dedicated to God. As I pondered what to write, the lyrics of "I Stand Amazed" came to my mind. The chorus goes like this, *How marvelous, how wonderful, And my song will ever be, How marvelous, how wonderful, Is my Savior's love for me!* Truly, I do stand amazed at all God has done for me. Ephesians 3:20-21 says it best,

> *"Now to HIM who is able to do immeasurably more than all we ask or imagine, according to His power that is at work within us, to HIM be glory in the church and in Christ Jesus throughout all generations, forever and ever! Amen!"*

God also must have known how much I needed you, Jay. You are such a pillar of strength to me with your steadfast love and faithful example of excellence. I could never express how grateful I am for your support and encouragement all along the way of the writing process. You are truly a blessing to my life.

To my sweet granddaughters, Abigail, and Elaine, who I can't wait to meet soon. I desire to leave a legacy of faith and love for Jesus as an example for you to follow, which is the most important thing I could ever give to you. I pray that you will love Him with all your heart, soul, mind and strength and this is something that you will never regret.

To my friends who have continued to encourage me to keep writing, thank you for your loving support. You bring a smile to my face and joy to my heart.

CONTENTS

301 YARD SALE

I used to love yard sales, especially when my kids were young, always looking for a bargain, but that was a long time ago. Several years ago, the 301 Highway Yard Sale became very popular stretching the entire length of 301. Last year I set up a table in our church parking lot to promote the REACH Mentoring Ministry and my first book. It was very hot and I did not have many folks stop by my table, as most people were hunting for some good deals. So, I tried to enjoy the shade, the breeze blowing as the cars drove by and the few people that did stop by my table.

One lady stopped by because of the sign for REACH, which is an acronym for Remember Encouragement Always Changes Hearts. She said she needed some encouragement and felt like God drew her to come speak to me. Her daughter had been in a car accident and had brain damage, which created a difficult home situation. I prayed with her, encouraged her as best I could and gave her one of my books. She said she felt lighter afterwards.

Another lady stopped by and she mentioned she probably had bought too much stuff. We laughed together, as we talked about how one person's trash can be another's treasure, but too often those new things can quickly become items in our next yard sale.

As we were chatting, I was reminded of the military yard sale I used to attend every year. I usually had a list of items I was looking for, but I began taking it to another level when I prayed about finding those particular items and to be careful about not bringing home things I did not need.

Well one particular year I found two specific items that although

I did not pray for, God knew those two items would totally delight me. The first item was a Tupperware cheese ball container. The background story was that many years prior, I hosted a Tupperware party strictly because I wanted the hostess prize. However, because my total sales were so low, I was not eligible to win it, nor was the host willing for me to just pay for it, which frustrated me at the time. When I spied that cheese ball container brand new and still in the plastic bag priced for a quarter, I became so excited. Just a simple thing, but I knew God was smiling over me.

The next item was a game called Mille Bornes. My family had spent many hours playing that, but I could not find it in the stores at that time. When I found the game in perfect condition I was thrilled to give the requested fifty cents.

When I went home, I was a happy little lady. I was in awe at God granting simple desires of my heart even when they are not that important. I believe that He blessed me because I asked Him to guide me as I made my purchases. He loves to be invited into every area of our lives and in turn He blesses us more than anything we could have imagined!

Psalms 37:4 says,

> *"Take delight in the Lord and He will give you the desires of your heart."*

I have experienced God's blessing over and over when He has said yes and even when He has said, "No." I am thankful that I have walked long enough with Him to trust that He loves me no matter what comes my way and that He is good. I am confident He has my best in mind even when I do not understand or like the circumstances.

Just as we shout "Coup Fourre'" in the game of Mille Bornes when we have a special card, so we should say "Thank you, Jesus," when He does amazing things in our lives. And if anyone would like to learn how to play the game, I would love to put a date on the calendar.

A VERY QUICK ANSWER TO PRAYER

After I had graduated from high school, I knew God wanted me to attend the Word of Life Bible Institute in Schroon Lake, New York. When I arrived there, I was so thrilled to be surrounded by God's beautiful creation and immersed in such a nurturing environment. I felt like I was in an incubator which helped me grow in the Lord.

Although I had been raised in church, answers to prayer were not a common conversation in my home. Most of the prayer meetings I had been a part of were usually praying for health needs or very vague, generic topics which made it difficult to experience a direct answer from God.

After I accepted the Lord at the Bill Rice Ranch camp (BRR), I immediately experienced God moving in my life which was really the first time ever and directing me to a Christian high school. The second significant answer to prayer happened after I had been at WOL for a couple of months which devastated me.

My prayer request was about a guy I met at the BRR where I got saved. We began a long-distance relationship since he lived in Tennessee and I was in Ohio. I was only sixteen while he was nineteen and he wanted me to move to Tennessee and get married. Well, because I was scared of moving and making that commitment, we eventually broke up after over a year of dating and visiting back and forth. I still believed that I loved him, and he stated he loved me as well and so in my heart, I always hoped that God would bring us back together one day.

After being at Word of Life for several months, I began thinking a lot about him. Because those thoughts were so persistent and occupying my mind, I decided one Sunday that I would spend the afternoon praying and seeking God for an answer. I asked God to reveal to me if I was wasting my time waiting on this relationship and I needed to move on, or if he was the guy for me. I let God know that I really needed to know what to do.

God did not wait very long to give me an answer. Back at my dorm later that evening, I was called to the pay phone: my sister, Bonnie, was calling. During our conversation, she mentioned that she had spoken to this guy's mom who told her that he had gotten engaged. Wow! God responded, but it was definitely not the one I wanted. I bawled like a baby because my heart was broken but I was touched that God responded to my request immediately.

God began comforting me and my faith in Jesus grew because I experienced His awareness of my situation when He answered my prayer almost instantaneously.

That was the beginning of my practice of praying specifically, because then the answers are obvious and clear. I have a long way to grow in my prayer life, but I am so thankful for all the ways God has worked in my life and in others as a result of my prayers. You can do the same! Start today! His line is never busy!

> *"Call to me and I will answer you and tell you great and unsearchable things you do not know.'" Jeremiah 33:3*

ANOTHER AMAZING BIRTHDAY GIFT

I In my first book, *It Makes Me Want To Cry When I Consider The Goodness of God, Volume I,* I wrote a devotion about the birthday gift that I did not want. Since then, God did give me an amazing gift on my birthday that I did desire. Here's what happened:

In 2020, my mother-in-love was trying to sell her house so that she could move closer to us. I am pretty confident everyone remembers how difficult that year was. Her house had been on the market for a while, but there was no action with the realtor and she was getting discouraged. I reminded her that she only needed one buyer. God was aware of her situation, and we could trust His timing. She also had concerns about where she would be able to move to. We prayed together and committed to trust God had everything under control.

Two days later on April 23, 2020, she received a cash offer on her house. On the same day, on the way to my birthday dinner, we saw a townhome for sale, just one minute away from our home. We called the realtor and made an appointment to see it the next day. It was perfect for her, and she made a cash offer on her beautiful lake townhome.

We received a call the next day from the realtor that another couple had also made an offer on it, and they gave us an opportunity to make another counteroffer without any information about what the other couple had offered.

My mother-in-love increased her offer. I felt led to write a letter to the owners about how wonderful mom was, how their beautiful home was perfect for her needs and how wonderful it would be to have her so close to us.

We received another call from the realtor, and he told us that her offer was not as much as the other one, but because of my letter, the owners would sell it to her, if she was willing to match their offer.

Thankfully, she was financially able to do that, and she signed the contract and moved in shortly after that. I will be forever grateful for the gift of Mom Stem in my life with such close proximity. I am also thankful for God leading me to write that letter that turned the owner's hearts toward her.

> *"He (God) determined the times set for them and the exact places where they should live." Acts 17:26b*

Father, thank you for hearing our prayers, and giving us what we need at exactly the right time. I am so incredibly encouraged to know that You know each of us and every single detail of our lives so we can completely trust You even when we are in the waiting room of life.

ARISE AND SHINE

A couple dear friends, Amy and Cary, encouraged me to listen to a podcast by Jaimie Winship. Since listening, I have been addicted to hearing his amazing stories of how God worked in his life. Jaime began asking God two questions: what did God want him to know? And what should he do? Then he waited and listened to God's responses. As a result, Jaime was very successful in his police work and began to receive recognition by others in similar fields of work.

Since listening to him, I have also begun to ask God these questions, but the hard part is listening long enough to hear God's response. Another question Jaime challenged us is to ask God what He calls you individually, or what He would call you as He tucks you in bed. Well, I have been asking, but I have not heard anything until today.

I decided to look up what Susan means and it said lily, but in the Hebrew, it means purity, beauty and innocence. My middle name is Elaine, and it means sun ray, shining light or bright. I realize that my life does not always reflect a pure shining one, but that is definitely my goal. Matthew 5:16 says,

> *"Let your light shine so that others will see your good works and glorify your Father in Heaven."*

Jesus called Himself the light of the world in John 8:12, and then He told the crowds that we are also to be the light of the world in Matthew 5:14.

Proverbs 4:18 says,

> *"The path of the righteous is like the first gleam of dawn, shining ever brighter till the full light of day."*

So, if you are wondering what God's will is for your life, here it is in John 6:40,

> *"For my Father's will is that everyone who looks to the SON and believes in Him shall have eternal life."*

Today, as I write this, I see the world becoming darker and darker, but God continues to remind me that darkness cannot exist in the presence of light. So, we must be intentional to follow the instructions we read in *Isaiah 60:1 says,*

> *"Arise, shine for your light has come, and the glory of the Lord rises upon you."*

Let God use you and you will be amazed at all He accomplishes through you as His conduit.

ARMOR OF GOD = JESUS

Several years ago, our pastor was teaching from Ephesians 6:10-18 and the importance of putting on the whole armor of God so that we will be prepared and equipped for the spiritual battle we are in. I have tried to break it down for more clarity below.

WHAT is our goal? Verses 10-11

"Finally, be strong in the Lord and in His mighty power. Put on the full armor of God so that you can take your stand against the devil's schemes."

WHO are we fighting against? Verse 12

"For our struggle is not against flesh and blood, but against the rulers, against the authorities, against the powers of this dark world and against the spiritual forces of evil in the heavenly realms."

WHY are we fighting? Verse 13

"Therefore, put on the full armor of God so that when the day of evil comes, you may be able to stand your ground, and after you have done everything, to stand.

WHEN should we fight?

"Be prepared in season and out of season." 2 Timothy 4:2

HOW can we fight successfully? Verses 14-18

- *With the belt of TRUTH buckled around your waist*
- *With the breastplate of RIGHTEOUSNESS in place*
- *And with your feet fitted with the readiness that comes from the gospel of PEACE*
- *In addition to all this, take up the shield of FAITH, with which you can extinguish all the flaming arrows of the evil one*

- *Take the helmet of SALVATION*
- *And the sword of the Spirit which is the WORD OF GOD*
- *And PRAY in the Spirit on all occasions with all kinds of prayers and requests. With this in mind, BE ALERT and always KEEP ON PRAYING for all the saints.*

He said something that I had never considered before. He said that each piece of the armor actually equates to who Jesus is. This led me to do a little research on my own and here is what I found in God's word.

JESUS is our TRUTH - *"Jesus is the way, the TRUTH and the Life…" John 14:6*

JESUS is our RIGHTEOUSNESS - *"This is the name by which He will be called, The Lord our Righteousness" Jeremiah 23:6*

JESUS is our PEACE - *"For He (Jesus) Himself is our peace." Ephesians 2:14*

JESUS is our SHIELD - *"The Lord is my strength and my shield." Psalms 28:7*

JESUS is our SALVATION - *"My soul finds rest in God alone; my salvation comes from Him." Psalms 62:1*

JESUS is the WORD OF GOD - *"The Word was God." John 1:1b*

This has been so encouraging to me ever since then and I hope it will be to you. Jesus is the Only One who can make us strong, firm and steadfast in the battles we face. So, don't leave home without Him!

BETTER THAN PLANNED

If you have known me for any length of time, you know that my life has not turned out as I would have planned. I, like any other little girl, had dreams of living happily ever after, like the movies portray, but God had much bigger plans in store for me.

I have to acknowledge, as God began to unfold some of the plans He had for me, I was not a happy camper. I spent a lot of time crying, praying and begging God for intervention and deliverance. I truly thank God for the dear friends that supported me all during those tumultuous years by being willing to pick up the phone time after time to help me process the pain. They did not always tell me what I wanted to hear, but they lovingly pointed me back to Jesus and encouraged me to work on myself and what I could actually control.

God used my friends, His Word, prayer, worship and every single struggle to transform me just like a caterpillar that has to be tightly shut in a dark cocoon for a time, only to emerge as a beautiful butterfly in the perfect time. God is still not finished with me yet, but I am definitely not the same person I used to be. Today, as a result, I enjoy a personal and intimate relationship with Jesus that I would never have experienced without the refining process. God taught me that there is a vast difference between a head knowledge and a heart relationship, and I am so thankful that God has connected my head and heart together.

I am grateful to say as I review my life thus far, it is better than I could have imagined even with all the struggles past, present or future, that I have either made it through or continue to wrestle with. God has been so gracious to me in allowing me to know

Him and use me for His kingdom purposes.

2 Corinthians 4:7-18 describes all the hardships we endure. Verse 10 states the purpose of our suffering which allows the life of Jesus to be revealed to others. Verse 17 states,

> *"For our light and momentary troubles are achieving for us an eternal glory that far outweighs them all."*

This is why I can testify that my life is way better than I planned. God knows me and loves me and has used it all to make me look more like Him!

So, when your life is not like you planned, trust that God loves you and that His plans are for your good and not to harm you. Ask Him to help you through the pruning process so that your life will produce beautiful and delicious fruit and accomplish the purpose He has for YOU!

BIBLE BEFORE BREAKFAST

Kings Jewels is an amazing discipleship program for children ages 4 – 10 years old. My sons were a part of this ministry, and we have fond memories of all the years they attended.

Well, now that my son has a daughter named Abigail, she was invited to participate in the camp out, which is the highlight of the year. The staff make it very easy by providing all the meals, activities, crafts, so each family is only responsible to bring their tent and camping supplies.

When I heard that they would be attending, I got excited and asked the staff if I could help out in any way during that weekend. I was surprised when they responded by asking me if I would present the Bible Before Breakfast devotion. I really did not know what might be appropriate, but they told me their theme was "When God Speaks." I told them I would consider it and pray about it, but I did not actually commit to doing this immediately. I also figured they had someone else in mind to speak since I was asked just a week before the event.

With only a week to pray and prepare, although God gave me a couple ideas, nothing seemed to be coming together. Finally, on Friday morning I called and told them that it was just not coming together smoothly, and I didn't think I was the best choice. They quickly encouraged me to just share some of my past stories, or even some of the devotions from the book I had already written. They talked me into it and so I agreed to share what I had at 8 am on Saturday morning.

That night, I reviewed my notes again and prayed that God would help me through this, bring it all together and speak through me and then I went to bed.

Saturday morning at 5 am God woke me up and began to speak to me about what to say and the order in which to share it. I knew I better get up and write it down before I forgot what He was depositing in my spirit.

So, I got up and when I finished writing all of the notes down, I showered, got ready, prepared my blueberry coffee and left my house around 7 am. I arrived 30 minutes early and was excited about how God had spoken to me.

When all the group was gathered, I shared with them what God had shared with me. Everyone interacted with me and I could tell the group was not only engaged but it was really ministering to their hearts when I saw tears in some of their eyes. Only God could have accomplished this because when God speaks, He touches hearts.

Afterwards, one of the staff moms said that it was the best Bible Before Breakfast devotion in all the seventeen years that she had attended. To God be the glory, great things He has done! I pray all the time that He will use me as a conduit that allows God's love to flow to others, and I believe He answered that prayer on that occasion!

> *"Whoever believes in me, as the Scripture has said, streams of living water will flow from within him." John 7:38*

BROWN BAGS

One of my favorite Christmas games is the White Elephant/Secret Santa game especially if I get the highest number. I guess this is a little selfish on my part because I like to see what everyone else has gotten before I pick my favorite choice. This game can be really deceiving since often a beautifully wrapped gift could actually contain a dead fish (true story) and an unlovely wrapped package could have the most lovely and expensive gift. I wonder which one you would choose? We learn quickly in that game that the outside is not the most important thing, but sadly, too often in life, we miss this truth.

Similarly, most people would agree that God is good when everything is going well in our lives, but how easily our perspective changes when our circumstances become unpleasant. Way too often we forget that God is still good and that He loves us even in the painful seasons. We struggle with God being fair, we compare ourselves with others, we throw ourselves a pity party, and we become depressed. Often anger at God manifests when we believe He has the power and authority to change situations, but He doesn't.

I completely understand these emotions, because I have experienced lots of painful times. Matter of fact, I occasionally still do this, even though I have experienced some of the greatest blessings in my life out of the ashes of burned-out dreams.

Philippians 1:10-21 talks about the Apostle Paul in the Bible who experienced so many hardships and ended up in prison for sharing the good news of Jesus. He responded that God had used every single painful experience to further the gospel and so he actually rejoiced because God was using his pain for others gain. Some of his last words were expressed in verse 21,

> *"For me to live is Christ and to die is gain."*

This is a profound statement, and I am so thankful for the examples in the Bible that we can model our lives after and learn to trust God when our lives seem to be so ugly and drab like a brown paper bag.

DECISIONS IMPACT DESTINY

When I was fifteen-years-old, I attended the Bill Rice Ranch Camp with my youth group which changed my life. Now, I had been raised in church, so I knew about God, but it was there that my head knowledge moved down to my heart and I accepted Jesus.

God began helping me to make changes so I would be more prepared for all He had for me. I began attending a Christian school to help me grow in my faith and I chose to only listen to Christian music.

I heard about the Word of Life Bible Institute located in Schroon Lake, New York. They also had summer camps for kids, and their Bible and counseling training helped to equip students to counsel the campers along with other ministry opportunities. I believed God wanted me to attend there so I began saving my income from my three part-time jobs at that time. I desired to help others who had no hope in their lives. This became very important to me especially when I kept hearing about all the young people that were jumping over the bridge in Akron, Ohio to end their life. I had to cross that bridge on my way to school, and it just broke my heart.

I attended Word of Life in the spring of 1983 and God began doing a deep work in my heart. By the fall, I met a guy and we began dating and quickly spoke of marriage. I had some concerns about our relationship, but I never sought out godly counsel. I also knew in my heart that my parents did not approve, but I proceeded with the relationship, moved to North Carolina and married in 1985 and seventeen years later got divorced. Talk about a bumpy road!

I ignored the warning signs and instead focused on my excitement of getting married and my dreams for my future. Well, similarly, if you are driving down a road with warning flags, but you chose to ignore them because you think you know best, you will probably end up in a bad situation. God is faithful to guide and direct us, but if we refuse to listen, we will surely suffer the consequences.

I am so grateful God is a Restorer and Redeemer of all our brokenness. When we get off track, He lovingly guides us back to Him, but I can tell you the process can be very painful. I love word pictures and this makes me think of a stained-glass window. God takes all our shattered pieces and can still make a beautiful picture out of our lives.

So, if you have made a bad decision, stop right now! Do not keep going! Pray and ask God what to do next. If you keep your eyes on Him, trust and obey His instructions, He will be faithful to guide you back onto His path for you. If you are already living with painful consequences of your choices, trust God to help you each step of the way and obey Him moment by moment. He will do what He promised in Psalms 30:11-12:

> *"You turned my wailing into dancing, you removed my sackcloth and clothed me with joy, that my heart may sing to you and not be silent. O Lord my God, I will give you thanks forever."*

DO NOT QUIT

In 1989, we became the house-parents for the Christian Life Home in Raleigh for pregnant, unwed girls. I was so excited and confident God had called us there. I felt like God was fulfilling His purpose for our lives. I had high expectations and expected the girls to be appreciative for all we were doing for them and the sacrifices made. Well, that was very short-lived, because our reality presented an entirely different perspective.

I was only 21 years old, not much older than the girls we would be taking in. Our first girl was only 15 years old, but boy oh boy, was she a challenge. She thrived on making our lives miserable. I did not understand the concept back then, that hurting people hurt others. I was young and eager to serve, but my self-confidence and faith was being battered every single day.

I went out for a daily walk, honestly, just to have a break and pray and cry. During those times, I begged God to let me quit. I let

Him know that this was way more than I felt like I could handle or even wanted to handle. I don't remember how many days or weeks I felt like this, but I know one particular Wednesday, I had had it! I was done!

That same evening, I attended the Wednesday night church service at Midway Baptist Church, and the title of the pastor's message was 'DO NOT QUIT!' How did he know exactly what I needed to hear? I was more than ready to throw in the towel along with my resignation. The scripture he used was from Acts 18:9-11:

> *"Do not be afraid; keep on speaking, do not be silent. For I am with you and no one is going to attack you and harm you, because I have many people in the city. So, Paul stayed there for a year and a half, preaching the Word of God boldly among them."*

Here is what I realized: I was afraid. I did not want to speak, rather I wanted to hide in my bedroom. I felt like I was being attacked by this young teen and I did want to entertain any further disrespect. I did not want to stay there another day, much less another year. Lastly, I was far from being bold.

But God! He had spoken to my heart and now I had a choice to make. Obey His voice or leave the home. Thankfully, God infused me with enough strength to let our Director, Amy, know that we would remain there for eighteen months just like Paul, and I would be praying for boldness to continue speaking life and truth to these girls.

God intervened on my behalf, and this girl was finally asked to leave the home because she just would not cooperate or comply with the rules. I am thankful to share that several years later, she called to apologize for her bad behavior and thank us for all that we tried to do for her.

I am thankful that God can bring a harvest if we remain willing to sow seeds of love and water them, no matter how difficult seasons can be. Father, please continue to use me to touch others with your love and help me to not give up and quit.

7/2/89
a.m.

GUIDED GROWTH

with Pastor James L. Upchurch

TOO SOON TO QUIT

Acts 18:1-17 — Acts 17:18 - calling Paul's names - making fun, scorning
Satan tries to wound our spirits.

II. Tim. 1:7 - "For God hath not given us the spirit of fear; but of power, and of love, and of a sound mind."

I. Jn. 4:18 - "There is no fear in love; but perfect love casteth out fear; because fear hath torment. He that feareth is not made perfect in love."

I. THE PROMISE OF HIS PRESENCE - "I AM WITH THEE"
though Paul was defeated in heart + head - He did not quit. Paul continued!

II. THE PROMISE OF HIS PROTECTION - "NO MAN ... SHALL HURT THEE"
Rom 8:31 - "If G be for us, who can be against us?"

III. THE PROMISE OF HIS POTENTIAL - "I HAVE MUCH PEOPLE IN THIS CITY" - Vs. 18
I have potential!
His grace is make perfect in my weakness.
2 Cor 12:9, Rom 8:26, 1 Cor 1:25

ACTION TO TAKE:

1. Get close to Jesus through prayer, G's word, praising G.
2. No fear in love - I. Jn. 4:18
3. Pray for God's presence
4. Look at others through the eyes of Christ

DO YOU KNOW HIS VOICE?

Jesus said his sheep know His voice and they will follow Him. I know that I am God's sheep and He is my Shepherd, but I am sad to say that I don't always follow His voice and obey His instructions. I am, however, thankful that I am learning to recognize His voice and can tell the difference between His voice and the enemy's voice.

Many years ago, when I was in a challenging time as a single mom both of my sons were part of the Cross-wave Youth Group which met monthly in Raleigh. I will be forever grateful for their investment in my son's lives.

Mary, one of the leaders, had a beautiful heart to minister to all the young people. She was very aware of my situation and after one of the meetings, she offered for me to take the food leftovers home after their weekend meeting. I was very blessed as God was continuing to show his faithful provision for our family.

We also talked about John 10 where Jesus spoke about being the Good Shepherd and that we are His sheep. Verse 3-4 says:

> "*He calls His own sheep by name and leads them out...and His sheep follow Him because they know His voice.*

Mary shared with me what had happened during one of their worship times. Benjamin went to Mary and he told her that he had heard God speak to him, that "He (God) was his Father." I began crying as this was so incredibly precious to me because I knew he was really struggling with feeling loved and accepted. God knew he needed those words of love and affirmation and spoke straight to his hurting heart reminding him that he belonged to His Heavenly Father.

This story continues to give me confidence to trust God when life is hard and we can't see anything positive ahead of us and our situation. God is our Good Shepherd and He loves everyone of His sheep. He is able and willing to meet us where we are and speak life giving encouragement to those we love and are concerned about.

Thank you, Jesus, for letting us hear your voice, being our Shepherd, taking care of our every need with Your amazing provision.

I'm not sure where you are today or if you know that Jesus is a real good Shepherd, but I challenge you to call out to Him. Pray and seek Him and then listen for His voice. He will respond but remember to trust Him even when He doesn't answer the way you asked. He knows you and He wants to give you the very best even though it doesn't seem like at the time. He is always faithful to take care of His own.

DREAMS

I have had many dreams in my life and honestly, I dream pretty regularly. Most of them seem crazy to me and others when I share them, but some of them have had great significance in my life.

Some have been about specific people that I may not have thought about for many years. If I was not able to reach out to them, then I would just pray for them because I believed for some reason, God put them in my mind and heart.

> *"For God does speak, now one way, now another, though it may not be perceived or understood; in a dream, in a vision in the night when deep sleep falls…" Job 33:14-16*

The verses go on to say that dreams are given usually to warn people.

God gave dreams to many people in the Bible as well. Joseph, for example, had dreams that I think helped to give him hope when he was sold as a slave by his brothers and later unfairly thrown into prison for many years. The Egyptian Pharoah, his butler and baker all had dreams that foretold events that would happen in the future. Joseph, the earthly father of Jesus, was given a dream about accepting Mary when she was impregnated by the Holy Spirit and was later warned about escaping to Egypt and when to return. Daniel had dreams about future events as well as the Apostle John. Peter had a vision/dream about accepting everyone that God calls into His kingdom and I am sure there are many others I have missed.

I definitely don't remember all the dreams God has given me, but there are a few that have been pivotal in my decisions and choices.

Once, I dreamed about an old high school classmate and as I prayed for him, I felt like God wanted me to attend my high school reunion so that I could share how God has worked in my life. I did attend and though I did not have lots of opportunities to share, I felt like I obeyed what God wanted me to do.

I had a dream not so long ago about four girls at my elementary school who lived in tough situations and needed support. God used this dream to start our annual REACH Mentoring Ministry day camp. We had a wonderful time together with the girls and have enjoyed camp every year since with new girls.

I have had many other dreams where I felt like I needed to reach out to those I dreamt about just to say hello and give support and encouragement to them. I especially love it when the person responds that was just what they needed at that time and God blessed them through my obedience to God's promptings.

I realize that we may not always understand why we are supposed to do something that was heavily impressed upon our spirits, but I do believe God loves to use us as His conduits of love and will always bless our response to Him.

GOD IS MY TIMEKEEPER

Psalms 31:14-15a says,

"But I trust in you, O Lord, I say, "You are my God." My times are in your hands."

God is acquainted with all of our ways, and I experienced amazing evidence of this early one morning in 1983. I was the camp counselor for a whole cabin of girls at Word of Life Bible Camp. I was awakened when I heard someone call my name, but to my surprise all the girls were still asleep. I smiled and thought maybe it was God who knew I needed to get up a little earlier to spend some time with Him before our busy day began. I got up and enjoyed a sweet time of fellowship with Him that day. Though this has been many years ago, it has left a lasting impression on me that He knows me, my schedule and He desires for me to make time for Him each day so that I will be equipped to fulfill His purposes for my life.

So, since that day, I have never set an alarm clock. God wakes me up each morning at just the right time and I can testify that I have never been late to an appointment due to God not waking me up on time. Now, maybe I rolled over and went back to sleep, and ignored His reminder to get up, but He has always been faithful. Even during the days of my nursing clinical days when I had to be up so incredibly early, God always was right on time to gently wake me up. Psalms 139:2–3 says,

"You know when I sit and when I rise; you perceive my thoughts from afar. You discern my going out and my lying down; You are familiar with all my ways."

I am so thankful we have a Heavenly Father who loves us so completely and has complete awareness of everything about me, the good, bad and ugly. The Bible also speaks about how God even knows how many hairs are on my head. I know He must spend a lot of time just on me, because I have very thick hair and it is constantly falling out. It is truly amazing when we really stop to ponder God's amazing love and concern for everyone and everything in His entire creation. He truly deserves all of our praise and adoration. Father, I thank You for all your goodness to us! You are a good, good Father!

GOD IS FAITHFUL TO PROVIDE

While serving as house-parents at the Christian Life Home, I became pregnant with my first son, Benjamin. The girls loved me being pregnant at the same time, and it definitely enabled me to empathize with them, and we had a lot of fun together. Though we had a lot of growing pains during our ministry time there, we knew God had put us there and we were grateful He was using us to make a difference in the girl's lives as they were choosing life for their babies.

We were so excited to become parents, but this also meant that we would need to move since there was no room for children at the maternity home. So, our search began for a home very prayerfully and intentionally. We had planned for me to stay at home to raise our children, so this meant we had limited finances for housing with only one income.

Well, I found an advertisement for a new home in Clayton on an acre of land for $53,000, but after speaking to the owner, they said this was mismarked and it was supposed to be listed for $63,000. So, they said they would honor the ad, but we only had three days to decide if we were going to purchase it.

We asked a realtor from our church to check it out. He told us after looking at it, that if we did not buy it, he would. We received this as God's provision for us, and we closed on it six months before we even needed to move which gave us time to get it ready before the arrival of our son.

Benjamin arrived in November 1990, which was three weeks early, but thankfully God enabled us to be prepared.

When I look back over my life and see all of God's provisions that He has lavished on us, I just stand in amazement. He granted us the desire for me to stay at home and raise our sons by stretching our income and giving us the discipline to live below our means so that we did not have extra financial pressure. Matthew 6:32b-33 says:

> *"Your heavenly Father knows what you need. But seek first His kingdom and His righteousness and all these things will be given to you as well."*

Trust Him for He will NEVER let you down.

GOD IS LISTENING

Recently, I felt like God used me in response to other's prayers. It was so encouraging for me, as well as for those who had prayed and received an immediate response from God. Here's how it happened:

My husband and I were enjoying our individual devotional time together one Saturday morning. I felt like I should call my dear friend Donna to check on her and see how her recent doctor's appointment went. I asked Jay if he minded me calling her since he was reading, but he said to go ahead and call her.

She began telling me that the doctor had given her medication to take, but she was concerned about the side effects. She said she had just got done praying about whether she should take it and she asked God to let her talk to someone who had taken it and how they had responded to it. Well, when she mentioned that, I asked Jay about the medication that he takes. It was actually the same type of medication which he has been on for around ten years with no negative issues. She was overwhelmed with emotion and said that we were a direct answer to her prayers, which made me emotional as well.

What is also noteworthy to state is that just the week before, God had put Donna on my heart to contact. That is when she told me her current medication had stopped working and she had a doctor's appointment the next week.

A pastor's wife had once told me that when God puts someone on your heart, you need to reach out to them. God may have an important purpose with His prompting and so I have strived to respond and reach out to others over the years.

I believe that had I not listened to the Holy Spirit nudging me to call her earlier that week, I would have missed the pleasure of being part of the answer to her prayer.

Later that same day, Donna told me she felt peace to take the medication and prayed that God would give her confirmation about the decision, and she told me when she started playing her music, her favorite song came on by Jesus Culture, and the lyrics spoke about God always being with us. She was crying when she shared this. I am so thankful for such a dear friend like Donna and especially for God to be so tender and loving and responsive to our prayers. Psalms 34:17 says:

> *"The righteous cry out and the Lord hears them."*

So, be bold to call out to God for our needs and concerns. He loves to hear His children pray to Him. Always remember too, that He is God and He is always good even when He doesn't respond the way you ask. He does have your best in mind, but we will not always understand all His ways until we get to Heaven.

GOD IS LISTENING – PART TWO

I had another experience where I felt that God used me again in response to someone's prayer in the same week that I had written about in the devotion, God is Listening - Part 1. Here's how this one happened.

I took my sweet mother-in-love to the hospital early one morning for a procedure she needed. We had had the same receptionist previously, Tokovia, and enjoyed our brief time sharing with her and she actually bought one of my books.

After completing the registration, she mentioned again about her diabetic sister being in the hospital and needed prayer.

She said her sister and husband had built a home and the closing was scheduled for July 4. Well, on July 2, her sister's insulin pump malfunctioned, and it continued to give her insulin for six hours while she was sleeping. By the time that it was discovered, she had acquired brain damage and so now three months later, she was still in the hospital and preparing to go to rehab.

That morning, we were at the hospital, Tokovia had been praying earlier for healing for her sister and asked God to restore her life. She said she had also mentioned she was confident that just a word or a touch of the hem of God's garment could heal her sister, but she did mention what she had specifically prayed.

After she shared about her sister, I spoke and used the exact same word about God being able to restore and it could take just a touch of His garment. She got very emotional and stated that God was just confirming that He had heard her prayer and that He was using me to encourage her heart.

Tokovia just kept saying, "God is listening and we must claim the healing He is able to perform."

I proceeded to share how God has restored my life in ways that I did not expect or even pray for. I can see now that His ways were so much better than what I had actually prayed for. Often, He uses very painful situations to work out His purposes in our lives as well as others' lives and bring us all closer to Jesus.

I was reminded about the story of Lazarus and how Jesus waited four days to go visit his family. When questioned, Jesus stated that He was glad because it was for other's benefit and for God's glory to be able to raise his friend from death rather than preventing his death.

Even as I write this, it is so encouraging to my heart, as I have been walking through some shadows of death too, but I am thankful it is just a shadow. I am confident that God is the same God who not only raised Lazarus, but also His own Son, Jesus Christ for our salvation and for God's glory. He can do the same for me and you.

So, whatever you are going through, praying for, waiting upon, we can have the confidence that God is listening, and His delays are not His denials. Trust Him completely no matter what and you will NEVER be disappointed in the end. Romans 8:28 says:

> *"And we know that in ALL things God works for the good of those that love HIM and who have been called according to His purpose."*

GOD ORDERS OUR STEPS

One day, my sons and I went to a coffee shop in Clayton and we observed a couple studying the Bible together. I was so impressed that I proceeded to walk over to speak to them and let them know what a great example they were setting for all to see. They introduced themselves as Jeff and Jessie and told me they had just graduated from Word of Life Bible Institute. I also graduated from there, so it was wonderful talking with them. God used that discussion as a catalyst for our family to apply to serve that summer at the Word of Life summer camp in NY. All three of us were accepted, myself as a nurse, Benjamin as a lifeguard, and John-Mark worked in the dish-pit. We had a great time and made lots of fun memories together, especially the day John-Mark and I decided to canoe while Benjamin was working as a lifeguard. I will share more about that funny experience another time.

After our summer there, my desire was re-ignited for my sons to attend Word of Life Bible Institute. In my survival mode as a single mom, I had forgotten about that, but I am thankful that God had not and He made it possible.

After both Benjamin and John-Mark graduated from high school, they decided to attend together for a year before pursuing their individual career paths. Even though Benjamin postponed his education plans, God worked through that as well, so that the housing arrangements would be ready the following year at the perfect time.

It was not an easy year for either of them as they both encountered lots of challenges. I am confident that God used that time in their lives to implant the truths of His word in their hearts and He gave them the strength to complete the year. I'm so grateful for the love of supportive friends, great supervisors and even their work assignments. God provided exactly what they needed at the time. God demonstrated His love for my sons more than I could ever imagine! I am continuing to learn to give my children and grandchildren back to God and trust Him to care for them in the ways that I cannot. He only has our best in mind through the good times and the hard times. Psalms 37:4 says:

> *"Delight yourself in the Lord and He will give you the desire of your hearts."*

Psalms 37:23 also says:

> *"The steps of a good man are ordered by the Lord, and He delights in his way."*

GOD'S GOT THIS

Many years ago, there was a devastating health issue that arose in my family that was almost unbelievable for me to process or comprehend. My heart hurt so bad, I felt like I could actually have a heart attack and die. It's amazing to look back now and see how God had everything in control even back then. This gives me confidence when new trials come my way. If He can do it then, He can do it again.

I am beyond grateful to say that I had some very dear friends and coworkers that surrounded our family. They showed us love, support and prayers during that time and even into this present day. Their hearts hurt with me, and they were interceding in prayer on our behalf. One of those horrible days, my friend Kelly truly encouraged my heart.

She told me that as she was praying, God spoke to her spirit that He had everything under control. When she shared this with me, I began crying, trying to comprehend that God cared so much that He would respond to my friend's prayers on our behalf. I requested her to write this down, so that I would remember His comforting words. She wrote down, "God's got this!" Wow! May I never forget this truth!

So many times, when we are going through very difficult situations, we focus on the problem instead of the promises of God. In order to have peace, we must intentionally put our eyes back on Jesus and not on our circumstances. We have to learn to trust Him, that He is God and He is good. Jeremiah 29:11 also says:

> *For I know the plans I have for you, declares the Lord, plans to prosper you and not to harm you, plans to give you hope and a future."*

Jeremiah 32:26 states:

> *God responded to Jeremiah's prayer, also during a time of distress, with these words, "I am the Lord, the God of all mankind. Is anything too hard for Me?"*

In other words, He's got this! You can trust and depend upon Him to carry you through the storms of life!

GOD'S PRINCESS

Many years ago, I went through a very difficult experience which made me feel like an orphan but when God revealed His truth to me, I was changed! God turned that circumstance around in order to etch upon my heart that I am actually a Princess, no matter what happens in my life. God is a King and since I am His daughter, that makes me His Princess! I am so thankful for this truth I learned back then. God has reminded me over and over which enabled me to stand strong when other storms raged around me.

I went to visit my parents in New York since my dad had to have surgery and since the surgery was at the Burlington, Vermont Hospital, they planned to stay at their friend Sharon's home in Vermont.

When I first met Sharon, our hearts were instantly connected because of our love for God, our desire to bless others and we were going through similar situations in our marriages at that time.

Well, my parents had arranged a ride for me to return to New York so I could fly home to North Carolina, but after meeting Sharon, she offered to drive me and pay the additional cost to stay at the bed and breakfast that had been arranged for me to stay at so that we could spend more time together.

When we arrived, we were warmly welcomed into the beautifully decorated bed and breakfast. Specialty chocolates were laid out for us in the bedroom, luxurious bath items were supplied, and Sharon surprised me with a dress and Honeysuckle body spray. I was so grateful to share this lovely experience with her.

That evening as I was pondering the prior events that had made me feel so unwanted, God opened my heart and eyes to see that what Satan intended for harm, God meant for good. Just like Joseph spoke to his brothers in Genesis 50:20:

> *"You intended to harm me, but God intended it for good to accomplish what is now being done, the saving of many lives."*

God used this event to permanently inscribe upon my heart that I truly am HIS princess. God enabled me to recognize that HE had placed me in a "palace," pampered me with delicious chocolates and lavish bath items, clothed me with a new dress, enveloped me with Honeysuckle fragrance, and gave me a new dear friend. He withheld my immediate desires in order to give me so much more. Sometimes, what appears to be so unfair, is actually His blessing in disguise and I have never forgotten this truth.

May God give us eyes to see His fingerprints on our lives and a heart to trust God when things seem to be out of control, that God is working for our good and His glory and that we are indeed His Princess.

GRANDMA'S CANDY DISH

I loved going to my Grandma's house! She was always very welcoming, and she made me feel special during the time I spent with her. Some of my favorite memories were the sleepovers at her house and watching movies with her on our Sunday afternoon visits. I remember she always had Special K cereal in a glass canister on her counter. She had Zest soap in her bathrooms and rose scented air fresheners. Probably my favorite thing to do when I arrived at her house, though, was to check out her candy dish to see what kind of candy it contained.

My favorite was the chocolate stars or the bridge mix. Looking back as a kid, the candy was my favorite, and the dish was secondary, but the full candy dish represented to me is that she had thoughtfully planned for our visit.

After she passed, the only thing that I wanted was her beautiful glass candy dish with the golden markings. I always displayed it full of candy until the unfortunate day it broke.

Many years have passed since then, but after my sister and her family recently visited, memories of my childhood resurfaced, and I remembered Grandma's candy dish. I Googled vintage candy dishes and to my surprise, I found one identical to hers for $20 and immediately placed it in my shopping cart.

I wish I would have had more time with my grandma and ask more questions about her life. This had its challenges, since she had completely lost her ability to hear, so we had to write her notes and then she would respond.

When my grandma went into a nursing home, I was not able to see her as much since it was an hour away. I still enjoyed every visit with her, and we played the card game Flinch, and she always had "cheese curls" or some other kind of snack.

She was very loved by the staff there and they provided outings for the residents. One of them was at the local mall. She had never been on an escalator, so they took her in her wheelchair. At Christmas, she had the opportunity to sit on Santa's lap.

My grandma collected poems which I also inherited after my mom passed. Grandma memorized many of them and recited them for different activities for the residents. I am so thankful that she had such a positive experience there in her final days on earth, but most of all I am thankful that she knew Jesus so that she is now enjoying Heaven for all eternity. I know this for a fact, because as I was looking through her poem collection, she had written about how she had trusted in Christ and received the gift of salvation. What a comfort and blessing to know we will see our loved ones again in Heaven.

Although I am excited for the candy dish to be delivered and begin making more loving memories with my granddaughters, most of all, I want to leave a legacy of faithfulness behind so that they will come to know Jesus early in life so that we can all be together one day rejoicing in Heaven.

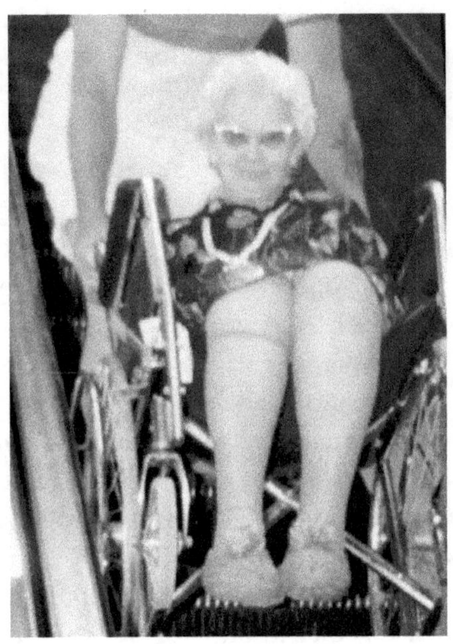

HOMESCHOOLING DAYS

Homeschooling is really like planting a garden. You need some good soil to plant the seeds into, fertilizer to help it grow and of course, water and sunshine to enable it to become strong, healthy plants and able to produce fruit.

When I first heard about homeschooling, I thought it sounded very strange. Then after I met some very wonderful homeschool families, my heart was opened to the idea, and so by the time my sons were ready for school, I was prepared to teach them. I am thankful God not only made it possible for me to stay home to raise my sons, He also provided several other families with which we formed a co-op group so that we could share lessons and learning experiences together. God used all of our individual strengths which helped to provide for a well-rounded education.

We made lasting friendships with the parents as well as the children. We met together to pray for our children and plan for each school year. We had so much fun together creating wonderful learning experiences for our children, but our ultimate goal was always to point them to Jesus and His amazing love.

Today, most of our children are raising children of their own and many of them are intentional in teaching them about God, His amazing creation, character qualities that will enable them to be successful in their world as well as from God's viewpoint. I am so thankful for this.

Though I was hesitant at first about accepting this opportunity, I am so thankful for the privilege of investing in their lives and the ability to enjoy quality time together. Those years were definitely not the easiest for me or my sons, but it was worth every single sacrifice and challenge that we went through during that season. I am so blessed to be Benjamin and John-Mark's mom, and I would do it all over again. Deuteronomy 6:7 says:

> *"You shall teach them diligently to your children, and shall talk of them when you sit in your house, and when you walk by the way, and when you lie down, and when you get up."*

Although we intentionally planted seeds in our children's hearts that would help them to grow in the grace and the knowledge of our Lord and Savior Jesus Christ, we are not guaranteed of the seeds taking root or a healthy plant. We must trust that just like it doesn't make sense for a daffodil to bloom when you have planted a sunflower seed, when we plant God's truth in our children's hearts, God is able to help those seeds to grow in His time and we must keep praying for them until they bloom!

I'M WATCHING YOU!

Many years ago, when I was a teenager, one of my relative's decisions and faithfulness deeply impressed me and I have never forgotten it.

My cousin, Bob Bevington and his wife June were much older than me, probably more around my parents age and had already retired.

Our families attended the same church and faithfully served in different capacities. Now, I am not sure how this exactly came about, but maybe a missionary from Bearing Precious Seed Ministry came to our church to share about their ministry and their hearts were touched by the Lord. They believed they were called to become missionaries with this ministry and began preparing to move to another area which led them away from their family and church friends. This was so impressive to me as they were pursuing God's call on their lives at the expense of living comfortably in their senior years and spending time with their children and grandchildren.

As they were preparing to move, my respect kept climbing for them. At that time, I was very involved in my youth group and was preparing to attend Bible college, and so I felt they also had a great deal of respect for me as well. Although I don't remember how this little thing began at church between us, but I would let him know that I was watching his life and testimony by saying to him, "I'm watching you!" and he would respond back with the same words, "I'm watching you too!" That was probably all we said to each other, but we both understood it meant so much more. It meant that we had utmost respect for one another and the faithfulness was recognized and acknowledged. I know for me personally, this was encouraging to me as a young teen to believe that an adult respected me.

The Bible says in Hebrews 10:24-25,

> *"And let us consider how we may spur one another on toward love and good deeds, not giving up meeting together, as some are in the habit of doing, but encouraging one another—and all the more as you see the Day approaching."*

This has been many years ago, and now both of them have been welcomed by Jesus into Heaven. I am confident they were so thankful they were obedient to God's call on their life to get the gospel printed and sent out all around the world so that others would also hear about the love of God. I am sure every single sacrifice they made was nothing compared to the rewards they received upon their arrival.

So, in your life, be faithful and obedient to God. You never know who is watching you!

JUST TAKE A MINUTE

Recently, I was attending a school nurse conference and as the nurses were sharing stories I was reminded of the importance of showing kindness to the students. They need us to take time for them because it might be the only safe place they have.

God also calls us to sow seeds of love and kindness to everyone as we are Christ's representatives. Though we may never get to harvest the fruit produced from the seeds we sow into their lives, we need to continue to invest into their lives.

As I was pondering this, I remembered the day I had screened a young man for hearing and vision at my high school. I was very kind to him, gave him candy and tried to make him feel valued. Just as a side note, he appeared to be like a poster child for bullying, so I made a very intentional effort to make him feel safe and at ease while in my office. When I finished the screening, I sent him back to class. Just a short time later, he was back sitting outside of my office. Soon, the principal and other administrative staff instructed him to stay in my office until notified. I had no idea what or why this was happening and the student also stated he did not know either. He was finally removed and transported to a mental hospital. Apparently, a suicide note had been found in which he planned to take his life in one of the school stairwells that day.

I am so grateful that his plan was interrupted and he received an intervention to get help and support. I will never know if my kindness earlier in the day made a difference which kept him from carrying out his plan, but I am so grateful for the opportunity that God gave me that day to speak life and provide support and kindness. Jesus said in Matthew 5:40,

> *"Truly, I tell you, whatever you did for one of the least of these brothers and sisters of mine, you did for me."*

This means that when we minister to others, you have actually been doing this as unto Jesus Himself. So, the next time you have an opportunity to be kind and speak an encouraging word, don't hesitate to take that extra minute. You never know what they might be going through and how you may even save their life.

LIGHTHOUSE CHRISTIAN ACADEMY

When I was no longer able to homeschool my sons, my heart was distraught over where they needed to go to school. I did not have peace about placing them in public school, so I prayed fervently for direction. My friend, Lisa, told me about a new, small Christian school in Benson called the Lighthouse Christian Academy. After I met with the principal and staff, I knew in my heart that that was the perfect next step for my sons. I inquired about the possibility of scholarships, but they did not have any. I still registered them with no idea how I would be able to pay for it.

Before the deadline came for me to pay, I received a call from our dear friends, the Hemingway's, who asked me to come over. Sitting in their living room, Joe told me that they had received some inheritance money after one of their parents had passed. He said they wanted to use some of it to help pay for the tuition, but it was actually enough to cover the entire amount. I was astounded by their selfless and extravagant generosity and praising God at the same time. Now, they had three children of their own and were living on just one income since Sherry was staying at home teaching her children. I am confident they probably had lots of areas where they could have used this money, but instead they chose to give it away and invest it in my family. This is still so incredible and almost unbelievable! Jesus said that when you give to others, you are actually giving it unto the Lord.

Also, Proverbs 19:17 says:

"He who is kind to the poor lends to the Lord, and God will reward them for what they have done."

This was incredible but even more so is that this happened again the next year in the exact same way. Another one of their family members had passed and with their inheritance, they wished to invest it once again in my sons by helping to pay their tuition.

Although this has been many years ago, I still am overwhelmed when I think about this and I pray God is still heaping blessings upon their lives, their children and grandchildren. What a beautiful, godly legacy they are setting for the next generations. I feel confident God is still smiling over their willingness to share sacrificially with our family. I feel sure Sherry had an extra warm welcome when she passed into Heaven and I bet she has an even bigger smile than she had on earth too!

MIRROR, MIRROR

One time my sister, Cathy, was visiting me, she brought her magnifying mirror to put on her makeup, and told me it would change my life. I chuckled about her comment, briefly looked at it, but disregarded the value that she placed upon it.

Several years later, I rented a small house that only had one bathroom. My soon-to-be daughter-in-law moved in with me until her wedding and so I bought a magnifying mirror so we could both have a mirror to get ready with in the mornings.

Well, as I began to use it, I quickly recognized what my sister had meant. I was now clearly observing blemishes, wrinkles, smudge lines, etc. on my face which I had never noticed previously.

Shortly after this, I got married and moved to a new home. Although the lighting was great, I knew I needed to have a lighted magnifying mirror mounted to improve my vision and apply my makeup.

I laugh to myself now, wondering how the mascara smudges around my eyes appeared to others that I had never noticed before. (Just a side note, none of my friends ever mentioned or fixed the problem.)

Today, as my age is increasing and my vision is decreasing, I am so thankful for my mirror and honestly, I don't enjoy traveling without it. I have purchased a travel mirror, but it is not the same strength. I am always thrilled when a hotel has one mounted in the room and I evaluate the quality of the hotel by this one feature. I usually comment to my husband upon our return home how happy I am to be able to look in my mirror again but since he is a man of few words, he just smiles at me.

This reminds me of a Bible verse in James 1:22-25 which says,

> *"Do not merely listen to the Word and so deceive yourselves. Do what it says. Anyone who listens to the Word but does not do it is like someone who looks at his/her face in a mirror and after looking at themselves, goes away and forgets what they look like."*

This passage continues to say that those who continue to listen and practice what they have heard, will be blessed in what they do. Although I desire to be blessed, I regret to admit that I am often guilty of not taking heed to God's instructions for my life and instead doing things my own way, which gets me into trouble.

God promises to bless those who follow His plans and this is what I truly desire for my life. How about you? So, next time you look in the mirror to fix your face, remember how much more important it is to take time in God's word and then follow His instructions for your life.

MISCARRIAGE

In 1994, I had an unusual situation. I had missed my menstrual cycle and so I went to the doctor to find out what might be the cause. I was 100% sure I was not pregnant, but when they did the pregnancy test, it came back positive. I was shocked because there was no way that this could have happened. Anyway, I loved my doctor, and he joked with me about how these things happen, and we laughed together. Although I had not planned on any more children, nor did I understand how this could be, I accepted with joy the gift God was giving me.

When I went back for the next appointment, I was actually showing a little, but my stomach definitely felt squishier than it had in my previous pregnancies. When they tried to find the heartbeat, they were unsuccessful. I told them that although this was not expected, I had accepted it and did not want anything to happen to this baby. When I was taken to have an internal ultrasound, there was no heartbeat, nor was there a baby inside only the placenta. Apparently, either the baby died very early, or my hormones just played a trick on my body.

As you can imagine, I was devastated. They sent me home and scheduled me to come back for a D&C (Dilation and Curettage) surgery to remove the placenta. My emotions were all over the place, first taking in the news that I was pregnant and now I was not.

When I went into the hospital a couple days later, I experienced God's peace which calmed my heart. He knew what I could handle. I woke up to my sweet friend, Amy, who brought me a little lamb stuffed animal. It brought tears to my eyes, as I remembered the words of Isaiah 40:11:

> *"He tends His flock like a shepherd; He gathers the lambs in His arms and carries them close to His heart."*

Thank you, Jesus, for taking care of my little one, until we meet again!

MISS JANE

Miss Jane was a wonderful lady and by far my favorite Sunday school teacher ever! She never married which allowed her more time to invest in her students which she regularly did with her time and money. I sure wish she was still alive today for me to tell her how much she meant to me, and how thankful I am for her faithful and godly example.

There were many times she would invite some of us girls out to eat for lunch and then to her home for the afternoon. She would occasionally take us to the shopping mall and give us coins to throw into the fountains in the middle of the mall. One time we went to a movie together. She gave great prizes as incentives for us to memorize verses or Bible stories. I won a very nice trophy for memorizing the books of the Bible, which I still remember to this day.

I realize today how blessed I have been by having positive role models in my life. I have learned by their example about the value and importance of investing time into others' lives, especially young people.

I have tried to follow their examples by serving others as well. God has given me wonderful opportunities to bless others while I was a houseparent, a volunteer with youth organizations, a teacher in my church, homeschooling, as a nurse in the public schools, now leading the REACH mentoring ministry for foster and at-risk youth and trying to be the best Grams possible to our sweet Abigail and any other grandchildren that God sends our way.

No matter where we find ourselves, God has divine appointments for us to meet, and we can show God's love by our words and our deeds.

Make the most of every opportunity and follow the advice in Titus 2:7b which says:

> *"In everything, set an example by doing what is good, showing integrity and wise speech."*

There is an old song by Steve Green, entitled "Find Us Faithful" and one of the lyrics is, "Oh, may those who come behind us, find us faithful."

My goal is that Jesus will find me faithful, and I hope it is your goal too. We only have a short time on this earth, so make sure to make your dash count for eternity.

MR. FRENCH – ONE INCREDIBLE LIFE

Mr. French was an incredible man who loved Jesus and others! Recently, he passed into eternity, and I am sure that Jesus had a warm welcome for him as He came running to greet him! I am also confident that our Heavenly Father spoke the words we all want to hear on that day, "Well done, you have been a good and faithful servant of mine. Enter into my kingdom!"

I am speaking of what I know about this man, but unfortunately, I never had the privilege and honor to actually meet him. For you see, he never tried to get acknowledgement or a thank you for all he was doing behind the scenes anonymously!

Several years ago, I was asked to speak about the REACH Mentoring Ministry at New Life Baptist Church. I only had about ten to fifteen minutes to share before the preaching began. Afterwards, I spoke to several people and answered any questions they had about the ministry.

Although the congregation was small, I don't remember any of their names, so I am not sure if Mr. French was among them.

Well, shortly after the Sunday that I spoke, tithing envelopes began to appear in the offering plates with REACH on the outside of the envelopes, crisp $100 dollar bills inside, but no name to acknowledge the generous donor. Week after week, month after month, year after year this continued for a little over two years. I never had any idea who this generous, faithful supporter of our ministry was, until recently. Tonya, the pastor's wife, had mentioned that there had been a death in their church family, and she suspected that he had been the donor, since no more envelopes appeared. Then the Wednesday night after the funeral, his wife stopped by the church office and said her son had found an envelope with REACH written on it and asked if they knew anything about it. Apparently, all that time, she was not aware of his generous donations. Just amazing! Mystery solved!

Tonya told me that Mr. French was a very humble man and a retired plumber, but apparently, he had taken a part-time job so that he could help support the REACH ministry. This made me tear up as this story was related to me. This truly humbles me to think that God is using the REACH ministry to not only touch our young people's lives, but also those that hear about us and are willing to partner with us in the ministry by praying, volunteering and donating.

As I reflect back on the day I visited the church, I have no idea what the spoken words were that so deeply touched his heart and gave him the desire to give so sacrificially.

Although he did not receive an acknowledgement on this earth for his extravagant generosity, I only can imagine the huge smile on Jesus' face as He welcomed Mr. Bob French into His kingdom. I also wonder if Jesus might have said, "You did it well, Bob! You obeyed my instructions from Matthew 25:34-40 that I gave while I was on earth." Verse 40 sums it up like this:

> *"The King will reply, I tell you the truth, whatever you did for the least of these children of mine, you did it for Me."*

Matthew 6:3, also the words of Jesus while on earth says,

> *"But when you give to the needy, do not let your left hand know what your right hand is doing, so that your giving may be in secret. Then your Father, who sees what is done in secret, will reward you!"*

I am thankful for witnessing this amazing testimony and can't wait to thank Mr. French in person when I get to Heaven one day!

MY CUP OVERFLOWS

God's timing is perfect and when He provided me with a new job with the Johnston County Public Schools, I was indeed grateful. I had only been working as a school nurse for six months when my credit card and license was stolen. It was quickly revealed which student took it, but she confessed and agreed to return the cards and pay back for what she had charged. Now, she was already on probation, and I could have pressed charges, but she would have been in bigger trouble. Instead, I chose to forgive her and use this as a learning lesson about God's grace. I spoke at length with her and encouraged her that with God's help, she could turn her life around instead of continuing to make very bad choices that would land her in jail.

All of the school administration were very surprised at how I responded and shortly after this incident, the school staff voted to nominate me for the "LEADING WITH THE HEART" annual award and I was chosen as the recipient.

God's ways are so amazing. I can now see why God allowed the uncomfortable situation in my previous job so that I would be willing to move into the perfect job for me. I truly love being able to make an impact on the students' lives.

I am so thankful that God restores our lives and can turn pain into places of honor. He uses all the good, bad and ugly in our lives to conform us to look more like Jesus. God took my dry cup and filled it to overflowing.

Psalms 23 says,

> *"The Lord is my shepherd, I lack nothing. He makes me lie down in green pastures, he leads me beside quiet waters, he refreshes my soul. He guides me along the right paths for his name's sake. Even though I walk through the darkest valley, I will fear no evil, for you are with me; your rod and your staff, they comfort me. You prepare a table before me in the presence of my enemies. You anoint my head with oil; MY CUP OVERFLOWS. Surely your goodness and love will follow me all the days of my life, and I will dwell in the house of the Lord forever.*

MY DAD

One of the most stressful times of my life was during my time at Johnston Community College in the nursing program. And if the program was not challenging enough, my dad was struggling with bone cancer and was nearing the end of his fight.

My parents had moved back to Ohio to be closer to family during this time. I tried to visit as often as possible, but between nursing school, working, finances and single parenting, it was rare. On one of my visits, I was lying beside him on the bed since it was more comfortable for him, and I was attempting to work on some of my reading assignments. I was so stressed and through my tears, I told my dad that I wanted to quit nursing school because I felt so overwhelmed. He turned and looked at me, and I will never forget his encouraging words which put so much wind in my sails. He began reminding me of the many times I had set goals for myself and accomplished them. He told me he believed in me and he knew I could do it. He also told me how proud he was of me.

It truly is amazing how words can be so powerful. Solomon, the wisest king also says this in Proverbs 18:21,

> *"The tongue has the power of life and death."*

So, the next time you speak, make sure you choose life words, no matter who you are speaking to. You never know what someone is going through and you can either encourage them or discourage them. Hopefully, you will choose to be like my dad, who gave me the inspiration to keep going and not quit when it was so hard for me.

MY FRIEND, ROXIE

Back in 2005, I began nursing school, which as I have mentioned before, was some of the hardest years I've ever had. Almost everyone in our class had begun taking anti-anxiety medication. I was also a single mom, cleaning houses and trying to survive nursing school. I never made an A the entire two years I was in nursing school, whereas I used to be a 4.0 student. I was so stressed and I couldn't seem to get a hold of myself. I did not have any time for extra-curricular or fun activities and even my church attendance was at a minimum. I am so thankful for the many people who helped me out by transporting my sons to different activities.

Life was tough for me, and it is during times like this that you really realize who your true friends are. Roxie was one of those friends. Through her own struggles, she developed such a kind, compassionate and loving heart. She has delight when others succeed and she is quick to help others when they need a helping hand.

One of the beautiful ways she demonstrated this to me was when she began sending me notes of encouragement and cards in the mail. One of the cards she wrote lots of scripture references and she included little cards of encouragement. These were so dear to my heart. I doubt she can comprehend how those words of encouragement made such a difference in my life at that time. She was like a lifeline of hope to my heart and mind. She supported me which enabled me to keep running and not give up in the race of nursing. She helped me to continue to do my best and get back up when I got discouraged, just like IV infusions give life saving measures. I am so thankful for her friendship and her willingness to invest in our family during this time.

Dear Susan & Boys,

How's your day been?

Here are just a few verses to remember.
Some/most are about the Joy the Lord gives
us. Some made you stop and think and some
make you glad your a child of the Lord.
Hope these help in times of troubles.

With love,

Fanny B.

Psalm 30:5
Psalm 46:1
Psalm 138:8
Psalm 139
Psalm 140:1-3/6-8
Psalm 18:2
Psalm 55:22
Psalm 27:14
Psalm 9:10
I Thessalonians 5:16-18
Philippions 4:13
Joshua 1:9
Proverbs 18:24
Romans 8:38-39
Matthew 6:32-34
John 4:10
Deuteroomy 7:9
Romans 8:28
I Peter 1:7 (very good)
Ephesians 3:17-18
Psalm 100:4-5
Psalm 8:3-4

God also compares this life to a race and how we need to keep pressing on to reach the goal of pleasing Him! Philippians 3:14 says,

> *"I press on to reach the end of the race and receive the heavenly prize for which God, through Christ Jesus, is calling us.*

The Bible also instructs us in I Thessalonians 5:11 to, *"Encourage one another and build one another up,"* which Roxie has definitely done for me.

I'm so thankful for Roxie's friendship and I hope everyone not only has a friend like her but that we can all become more like her.

If you know a friend who is having a hard time, maybe you can share encouragement by sending a note, making a phone call or text, baking some cookies and making time to visit them. You never know how you could infuse them with hope and you might even save someone's life. We never really know what someone might be going through but decide today to make a difference and impact on others. You never know, you might just become a superhero to someone who is struggling.

OPEN AND CLOSED DOORS

I LOVE when God makes it very clear which way to go when a decision is required. Through the years, I have learned to pray that God will open and close doors, especially when I am not sure of the path I am to take.

> *"God says that when we lack wisdom, we can ask God and He gives it to us liberally." James 1:5*

I have experienced His leading many times as a result of my praying, and this is one of the testimonies I have regarding this.

I graduated from nursing school in 2007, and I wrote about in my first book how I obtained my first job, so I won't repeat that story here. When I began my job at the hospital, I truly loved caring for the patients there, but the stress grew very quickly as the patient load increased many days up to six to eight very sick and fragile patients. Because I was a new nurse, I was probably not as efficient, and I was exhausted on the medical/surgical floor. I began praying for a new job even before my first year was completed.

I applied to the Raleigh Rescue Mission, WakeMed—mother and baby, Johnston Health—postpartum, and also at the Johnston County Health Department as the communicable disease nurse. Every single interview seemed so promising, I thought I might get offered all of them, so I prayed that God would close the doors to each one except the one He wanted me to have and He did just that!

He actually slammed every door except the Health Department. The rescue mission never called me back. Women's Health filled the position with my friend, Andrea, who never even applied but they gave her the position just to provide her with pediatric experience required for her desired job. She was only in that position for four months, long enough to eliminate me. WakeMed disqualified me since I failed to respond to a survey at the end of the application and that left me with accepting that job as the Communicable Disease nurse. He knew exactly what I needed and I really did enjoy that job for ten years until… I didn't any longer.

When you pray specific and God answers specific, you can truly witness God's involvement in your life and what a personal God He is.

Jeremiah 29:11-13 reminds us that He knows the good plans He has for us and verse 12 says,

> *"Then you will call upon Me and come and pray to Me and I will listen to you."*

OUR AMAZING BEACH VACATION

I love rehearsing about God's amazing faithfulness in my life and our beach vacation was one I will never ever forget. John 1:16 says,

"Out of His fullness of grace, we have received blessing after blessing."

This was true for me and continues to be the story of my life.

Now, I will have to say that not everything that has happened in my life appeared to be a blessing at the time, but looking back over my life thus far, I now can see how God has used every circumstance—good and bad—for my good and His glory, for which I am thankful.

Our beach vacation plans began while I was cleaning at Shelly's home, and she left a note inviting me to use their timeshare that summer. I was very excited and so grateful for her selfless generosity which reminded me just how much God loved our family and how dear our friends were as well allowing His love to flow through them to us.

The blessings continued to multiply because when the principal from the Christian school my sons attended heard about this, she provided a gift card for groceries. Another friend, Amy, slipped me $50 dollars in my car for gas. When we arrived at the timeshare, we met some old homeschooling friends, Lauren and her children, and they had brought us additional groceries. We had a great time of fellowship and fun with them at the beach.

Lauren also invited us to eat spaghetti with them at their church Wednesday night supper.

I told the boys that we would only be able to eat out one time that week for lunch. We went to Captain Bill's Restaurant one day and while we were waiting for our meal, we were guessing the names of the United States on the placemat. A lady leaned over the booth and stated what fun it appeared we were having together and proceeded to ask us where my husband was. I responded that he had left our family recently. Her head immediately swung around and said that God would be faithful to take care of us and provide. I instantly responded that He already had been and that is why we were there now. She continued to encourage me with her kind words until we got our food.

After she finished her meal, she got up and stood in front of our booth. What she said next, still amazes me. She said, "You may think that I am crazy, but God has told me to pay for your meal today." We were all flabbergasted at this extravagance provision for our family since we did not even know her. I let her know that I did not think she was crazy, because we were experiencing the unbelievable goodness and provision of God over and over. We thanked her profusely and I got her name and contact information so I could send her a thank you note. Her name was Judy. After she left, all we could do was sit in silent amazement of how God sees us, cares for us and provides in unbelievable ways.

Finally, to top off our week, Lauren told me their church had extra tickets for the Avalon concert, and we were welcome to join them. Well, at that time, they were one of my favorite singing groups and the location was on our way home, so we were delighted to accompany them for an amazing concert. It was just like God had already given us this delicious ice cream sundae and then He placed a huge cherry on top to bless us with a grand finale.

It truly was a week of blessings upon blessings, and I don't believe any of us will ever forget it.

PREPARE FOR WHAT'S AHEAD

A wise woman once told me to prepare for what's ahead. At that time, my life was very difficult, but I tried to heed that advice, and God was faithful to direct my steps.

Then, three years after I graduated from nursing school in 2007, I felt God prompt me with the same instruction to prepare for what is ahead. King Solomon wrote in Proverbs 24:27 says,

> *"Finish your outdoor work and get your fields ready and after that build your house."*

In other words, prepare for what is next.

So, although I loved my position as the Communicable Disease Nurse at that time, I knew the nursing requirements were changing and I would eventually need to have my BSN if I wished to get another job. I honestly still felt traumatized by my nursing school experience, but I knew I needed to begin the journey.

Since I was not in a rush and I did not want to be too stressed out, I began by taking one class per semester. I am very thankful that my supervisor at that time allowed me to use my lunch hour to attend my classes at Johnston Community College. It took me four years to complete all the prerequisites and two more years for the BSN program. I think my picture might be beside the definition of a lifelong learner. I finally graduated in 2016 with my BSN.

I still had no desire to change jobs until I was required to add the additional role of STD nurse. I then pursued the school nurse position which required a BSN degree. How amazing is God! He had led me all those years to prepare me for what was ahead. I cannot tell you what a blessing it is to have confidence that I am exactly where I need to be. I love the ministry that I am able to have there and speak life, truth and hope to the students.

I am also actually thankful for the discomfort I experienced before I left because God used those very things to move me out and into the next and best chapter of my entire job career.

PUT IT BACK WHERE IT BELONGS

I LOVE my husband, Jasper Graham Stem, Jr.! God has done an amazing job of bringing us together and uniting our hearts in marriage and almost six years later, I still can't believe I am married.

I never had the privilege of meeting his dad, but I LOVE his mom dearly and thank God for the way they raised their children, Jay, Eric, Betty, and Kevin. They are all wonderful people, and I am grateful to be a Stem.

Through our years together, Jay has shared about his dad teaching him practical life lessons and ways to be successful in life. One of these is to put things back where they belong. He even said that if they did not return things to their designated home, they got in trouble. Jay learned this lesson almost to perfection. (We won't mention the key left in his pocket that one time.)

Anyway, as much as I appreciate this reminder, I did not have the same reinforcement in my home of origin. Therefore, I get to learn this the hard way, which really stresses me out when I cannot find something which I did not return to its home.

I really do have the best of intentions, but way too often, I get too many things going at the same time. Therefore, I fail to handle it at the time, and this definitely messes me up later.

I have learned through the years to ask God to help me find my missing items and I have to say that He is always faithful to help me, but not always the exact time I think I need it. I think He allows this so that I might learn the lesson hopefully the next time. My wise friend, Cary, told me something I have never forgotten: we learn more from pain and failure than success.

I realize this verse is taken a little out of context, but I want to place it here. I Corinthians 14:40 says,

> *"Everything should be done in a fitting and orderly way."*

So, next time you set something down, make sure to go ahead and put it in its proper place and you will save yourself stress later. Trust me, I know this from too many experiences.

(PS. When I read this to Jay, he said to add that I am still a work in progress. LOL)

REFINANCE

Life was challenging when I became a single parent. I had no education, no job, no cushioned bank account and I had to refinance my home as part of our legal proceedings. This presented a real problem. Since I had chosen to stay at home and raise our sons, I did not have a working history; therefore, no company wanted to take the risk to help me to refinance our home. To put it mildly, it was a very stressful time. Finally, God led me to Bruce Braddy, and he agreed to refinance with an interest-only loan for only $200 a month. After three years, I would need to be prepared for a full refinance. This put some pressure on me, but I was trusting the Lord to work out all the details and the way I was calculating, I should be done with nursing school by then and have a job to support our family.

But surprises happen that send wave shocks into our best laid plans. One of these was the letter I received after applying for nursing school, stating that I did not get into the program and would have to wait until the next year to apply. I knew this would interrupt the three-year plan to refinance, but I reminded God that I did not have a Plan B, so He was going to have to help me out. I had to put into practice learning to trust God in the unknown and the uncertain, even though I had no idea how this would work out. But God came through once again.

The day before nursing school started, I received a call from the nursing program informing me that someone had dropped out and I was the next on the list. I did not have any of the prerequisites, so I was put on probation until I completed them. Even though I was behind, God helped me catch up quickly and remain in the program, although it was often questionable when I would fail a test. I studied very hard, but occasionally I would not pass even after studying many, many hours. I continually prayed and told God that I would do my very best, but if I did not make it, then He was responsible for a Plan B, because I did not have one. Praise God, He helped me every step of the way. Psalms 37:23-24 says,

> *"The steps of a good and righteous woman are directed and established by the Lord, and He delights in her way and blesses her path. When she falls, she will not be hurled down, because the Lord is the One who holds her hand and sustains her."*

I am so thankful for God watching over me and providing for me in just unbelievable ways. He truly has carried me through every single hurdle I have encountered and, in the process, changed my life.

PS. I did graduate from nursing school and was able to refinance my home within the three-year timeline. Praise the Lord!

SETBACKS WERE ACTUALLY SET UPS

When I was in eleventh grade, I was working hard in school and trying to figure out a way to graduate early. Sadly, the Christian school had some problems and half of the teachers left so I wasn't even sure I would be able to finish the classes I was currently in. God directed my parents to enroll me in a different Christian school in Akron, Ohio, which could provide all the courses I needed to graduate early. It was arranged for me to live with my twin sisters that year. Transportation to the school was provided by a local family, the Walker's, who were willing to drive me there along with their children. Most mornings, I would walk three blocks to their house in the mornings and afternoons to make it a little easier on them, since they had five children to get ready in the mornings. I had to walk by lots of students who attended the local public high school and so I tried to share God's love with them by smiling and passing out gospel tracts.

This happened early in the school year, so by the time I started the new school, I was already behind. I spent many hours every night doing homework, especially in accounting and shorthand to catch up since I had never taken those classes previously. Thankfully, I did well and actually graduated second highest in my class.

I did not appreciate all the changes during my senior year at that time, and honestly it made no sense to me but looking back now, I can see how God used what seemed like a setback to actually set me up for the future. For example, I was able to get a job in the incoming department at Word of Life Headquarters because of the accounting class. Later, when I moved to North Carolina, I was able to get a secretarial position at Carolina Power & Light Company because I had taken the shorthand class.

One other thing that God used in my life was our daily drive to school with the amazing Walker family. I loved our time together and I learned so much from Brenda and the way she and Wes were raising their children. We had to daily cross over the bridge which was nicknamed the suicide bridge since so many people were ending their lives by jumping over it. One day, we saw emergency vehicles there, due to another casualty. This broke my heart for young people and helped to plant the desire in my heart for caring for children in hard places. This puzzle piece of my life led me to serve in different youth ministries as a young adult and eventually to begin the REACH Mentoring Ministry for foster and at-risk young people.

Joseph in the Bible may have felt the same way earlier in his life when the bad things kept happening to him during his youth, but later in Genesis 50:19-20, he could clearly see how God had worked in his life through it all and he told his brothers,

> *"Don't be afraid. Am I in the place of God? You intended to harm me, but God intended it for good to accomplish what is now being done, the saving of many lives."*

Only God can take every single circumstance and use it so that we will be prepared to fulfill His purpose for our lives. I will never be able to thank Him enough for choosing me to be His conduit of love to others!

SHINING LOVE AND ENCOURAGEMENT

I had a friend who was always such an example of selflessly serving others in big and small ways. He would randomly do crazy things just to make others smile and let them be reminded that they were loved and cared for. Like the time he bought sweat suits for his sisters and put them in random places for them to find, like the refrigerator. Or sometimes he would write notes all over their mirrors in their houses or hide encouraging notes behind after visiting his relatives that they might not find until long after he had gone home. He was the friend that you would always want to be around.He wasn't ever choosy who he demonstrated love and kindness to; it could be a close family member or a total stranger.

Here's one of the examples that I have never forgotten: we had gone to Golden Corral, and we ran into some of my old acquaintances, and they had their great grandson, Joseph, with them. During the conversation, it was mentioned that Joseph loved tomatoes. This was just a random comment which I never thought about again until we left and headed straight to Lowes to buy a tomato plant for Joseph. My friend had no motive except to just surprise and bless him. We didn't deliver it that night, but not too long afterwards, we dropped it off on his front porch.

I have thought about this so many times and often wondered what Joseph's face looked like when he saw it since no one was home when we delivered it. It is amazing how just a small act of kindness can go a long way in the heart of another person.

I didn't even really know this little guy, except that I knew he had lots of challenges in his life, but I pray that he felt the extravagant love of Jesus through that simple gift. Jesus said in John 13:35,

> *"Everyone will know that you are my disciples if you love one another."*

I am sure that Jesus has smiled so many times over the random acts of kindness that my friend scatters wherever he goes. He always leaves a trail of thoughtfulness. It would be an amazing world if there were more caring people in the world like him!

SINGING IN THE RAIN

I was recently asked to pray for a friend's car issues and it reminded me of a frightening experience I had which led to me singing in the rain. Here's what happened:

I was driving on a very rainy Friday evening into Raleigh taking my sons to their youth activity. Well, on the way there, my windshield wipers began to have issues, and I had to keep pushing the windshield washer fluid lever to make the wipers work. I made it safely to the church where I needed to drop them off and then I immediately headed home.

By then, the rain had increased and it was completely dark. The wipers were just not working at all and sometimes even the washer fluid lever would not work to clear the windshield. It was just plain terrifying trying to drive in the pouring rain at night without the wipers working. I made it almost to Clayton when they quit working altogether. Believe me when I say, I was doing some serious praying to God for help. I pulled into a gas station and tried to call a couple friends, but no one answered.

Finally, I said, "Well okay God, it's just You and me," as I drove out of the gas station. I began singing the old gospel song, "Till The Storm Passes By." Miraculously, the wipers began working... until I stopped singing. I began singing again, and the wipers began working again. This pattern continued all the way from the gas station to my house.

The wipers continued to work until I pulled into my driveway and then they quit again. I was never so relieved to be home, nor had I ever appreciated working windshield wipers so much.

As I pondered this situation, I think so often we treat God the same way we do windshield wipers, we only talk to Him when we need something or we need His help. Jeremiah 33:3 says,

> *"Call to me and I will answer you and show you great and mighty things."*

May we all become more thankful and appreciative of His touch on our lives, not just in our crises, but every day of our lives. And don't forget to sing and give Him praise even in the midst of our crisis, for He loves to hear our voices lifted in praises to Him!

STEPPING OUT AND MOVING ON

I am so thankful for the people God places in our lives to encourage us to step out and make some needed changes. My son, Benjamin, is one of those people.

I had lived in the same house for many years and while we made some fun memories, there were also some very hard ones. It had never been my dream home, but I know that God had placed us there and financially it made sense to remain there especially after becoming a single mom. But after both of my sons moved out, I was ready for a change.

One time when Benjamin came home to visit, he encouraged me to look at some homes, and I found one I really liked. I got so excited I went home and put up a For Sale by Owner sign in my subdivision and yard the next day.

Although I had seen a home I was interested in, I knew I needed to get my asking price for my house so that I could afford it. Because I had already been experiencing God's amazing provision, I knew I could trust God to work out the details and therefore I was not stressed or felt rushed.

Well, I finally graduated with my BSN in May of 2016, and I got an offer on the house the next month. Unfortunately, though, the house I had my eye on, had already sold, so I began looking hard for a place to move without any success.

One day, I received a call from the Levin family, and they offered me to stay in their extra townhome that was unoccupied.

They told me they would like to help support the REACH ministry which was just beginning so they did not charge me anything, even though I tried to pay them. They did allow me to clean their house for them in exchange for me staying there.

While there, I continued to look for a place, but honestly nothing fit my needs nor my finances. After ten months of living there, I moved out and rented my dear friend, Anne's home after she passed on to Heaven. I knew it might be a short stay since it was for sale. It was a very stressful time for me but after praying about it, God gave me a peace that He would not let the house sell until He provided another place. I was also encouraged when I read in Acts 17:26b,

> *"He determined the times set for them and the exact places they should live."*

WOW! I was sure glad He knew where my next home was located because I sure did not.

Well, just a short time later, I received a call on my birthday from Anne's daughter, Luanne, who informed me that they received a cash offer and the house had sold and I would need to move within a couple of weeks. I was devastated and the tears just flowed down my cheeks in front of my sons who were with me in the restaurant. Later, she called me back and told me about a rental house that did not require me to sign a lease for only $700 per month. The next morning as I was preparing to go see it, I cried out to God, and said, "I sure know how it feels to be a foster child." He quickly reminded me that this was not true and that I could buy a house that day if I chose. I humbly agreed with Him. I went to look at the house, signed the agreement and began to move in. God was faithful to provide a home for me the same day that the house sold just like He promised.
It was an older renovated home that brought back fond memories

of my childhood home, and it was perfect for my needs at the time, and I am very thankful for His provision. I can also see now why God did not allow me to purchase a home during that season. God was just about to send me a handsome prince who already had a castle waiting just for me!

THE BEST BOSS EVER

Colossians 3:23 says,

"Whatever you do, work at it with all your heart, as working for the Lord, not for men."

I am trying to put this into practice in my life, and I have resolved to live my life with more excellence in all areas.

As I have pondered this, I was reminded of my boss, Paul Meade, who inspired me to become a better employee. We only worked together for a few short years, but his impact continues to influence my life with the lessons I learned from his life.

Paul was one of three bosses whom I worked for as a secretary at CP&L. I acquired my job through a temporary agency without having any formal training. Although I was doing my best, my lack of expertise must have been noticeable. No one ever criticized my work, but Paul must have recognized my potential and willingness to grow so he began giving me suggestions on how to better anticipate needs and what was expected of a secretary. He was always very encouraging to all of his staff, and it made all of us want to please him.

One of the simple ways he did this was that he began putting little stars and positive comments on work submitted to him by his staff.

He also took his team to lunch, brought in special treats for his staff, and celebrated their successes and accomplished goals. Team Building was important to him, and he created opportunities to connect not just with our team, but he often included our families. Even when deadlines were stressful, he remained respectful to all the staff working hard to complete the projects. He showed value to everyone and made them feel special.

Our paths parted when we both took different jobs, but our friendship continued. His career led him to Ohio where he lived with his sweet wife, Amy, and two daughters, Sarah and Katherine who he loved with all his heart and was completely devoted to. I was so happy to meet them when we visited my family in Ohio.

Paul Meade passed away many years ago due to cancer, but I will always be grateful for his investment in my life. His example of taking time to help others, motivating them to do their best, and working with excellence and making everyone feel special lives on with those who knew and loved him.

His legacy also continues to make so many people happy when they taste his amazing chocolate chip cookies which his family continues to bake (now named Mr. Meade's cookies) to carry on his one-of-a-kind delicious tradition.

So, if you are ever in the area of Cuyahoga Falls, Ohio, make sure you place an order so you can enjoy the best chocolate chip cookies yourself and I am confident you will not be disappointed.

THE GREEN GRASS IN THE MARSHY AREAS

As my husband and I were driving to the beach one time I saw tall green grass that looked like it was in the marshy areas, but then there were some areas where it actually looked like it had been mowed down. As I thought about this, I spoke to my husband, and he told me it was just where the tide had come in and out which made the grass lay down and brown out. I had wondered how in the world had it been able to be cut down so I was glad he was able to answer my question.

As we were driving, I continued to ponder the beautiful green grass that looks so lush and inviting to sink our toes in. While it looks like firm ground to walk on, there is actually no safety or security in walking through that area at all. I felt like God spoke to me about the similarity to the enemy's deceptive ways and enticements. Satan lures us with all kinds of temptations which look so inviting and satisfying to our fleshly appetites. However, after we indulge ourselves, we realize we are in deep trouble. There is nothing actually good about it at all and then to top it off, he hangs a shame sign around our neck for the decision we made.

In Genesis 3, Satan did the very same thing to Eve. He promised life when she ate the apple, but shame and death came instead. Satan uses the same strategy today on us as he did back then. His entire goal is to try to make us doubt the goodness of God and believe that He is holding out on us. He wants us to turn our hearts against God, the very One who loves us in order to take our attention off of our real enemy.

In John 10:10 Jesus said,

> *"I have come that they may have life to the full, the enemy comes only to steal and kill and destroy."*

So, the next time you see luscious green grass, make sure it has solid ground under it before you sit down. Also, consider when you get tempted to do something, think about the consequences of your actions. Make sure that you always remember that God is good, He loves you and only has your best in mind, even when He says, "No," or "Wait," which is usually for our protection.

THE POWER OF FORGIVENESS

Recently, I experienced something more powerful than dynamite. Now, dynamite is a powerful tool which can be used to destroy, but it can also be used to expose valuable minerals in the ground, and it can remove debris from a wreckage to possibly save a life. But I have learned over the years that forgiveness is even greater! If forgiveness is withheld, pain, bitterness and destructive forces multiply, but when forgiveness is generously given, peace, harmony and restoration can take place. I recently was blessed with the gift of forgiveness which brought reconciliation for which I thank God.

Several years ago, a dear friend of mine became offended at me due to a difference of opinion. We had never had an issue in all the years that we had been friends that I was ever aware of, so it was not only surprising to me when I realized how angry she was, but it also made me very sad and confused. Now, I am a peacemaker naturally, so I always strive to do my part to have good relationships. I was not even sure what the problem was, but I tried to take the initiative by bringing her lunch one day and called her on a couple of different occasions just to say hello and connect with her.

My goal was to provide an opportunity to show my concern and care for her but after that, I just was not sure what else to do besides pray about it as God brought the issue to my mind.

When I first became a Christian as a teenager, God reminded me of some friends that I needed to ask for their forgiveness. When I met with them, most of them were not even aware of the darkness I had in my heart towards them. They all gladly forgave me, and this action restored those friendships. I am so glad God taught me this powerful truth lesson many years ago.

Fast forward back to 2025 when I received a call from my friend. She asked me if I had a minute to talk, and of course I said yes! She then proceeded to tell me that she had been mad at me for the past five years, which I responded with, "I know."

She then told me why she had gotten angry, and she admitted that she had been wrong over the situation and asked me for forgiveness.

WOW!

She said she had been around some young moms and remembered her old friendships with fondness. Now, several of our mutual friends have passed on Jesus, and other friends might not be as close due to lots of other reasons. Anyway, she said how much she valued our friendship and that life is too short to hold onto a grudge or anger. I completely agreed with her. Life really is fragile and broken friendships are very painful, but boy oh boy, restored friendships are life giving and puts fresh air in our oxygen tanks.

God designed us to be in connection with Himself and others, so we have to be sober and alert to the tricks of the enemy that is continually sowing bad seeds in our hearts and minds. We must be intentional to rip them out before they grow up to choke out the love of Jesus towards those God has placed in our lives for a purpose. Colossians 3 says,

> *"Therefore, as God's chosen people, holy and dearly loved, clothe yourselves with compassion, kindness, humility, gentleness and patience. Bear with each other and forgive one another if any of you has a grievance against someone. Forgive as the Lord forgave you. And over all these virtues put on love, which binds them all together in perfect unity."*

THE STRANGER THAT RESCUED ME

God gave me a desire to help others early in life, but when I went through a very challenging season, I felt like I was on the receiving end instead for many years. God has finally brought me into a new season, for which I will continually praise Him. Thankfully, I am now much more able to be a channel of His love for others that are in hard places.

Recently, an aged-out foster girl reached out to me because her truck broke down and she needed help with transportation. I quickly remembered a similar situation I had experienced. I was happy to assist her and especially grateful that God had changed my role in this scenario.

Many years prior to this, I was driving my car home with my two sons, being fully aware that it had transmission issues which limited its ability to even maintain the speed limit. Well, I made the drastic mistake of getting on Highway 40 Interstate. I had my hazard lights on, so everyone was going around me. It did not become a serious problem until I exited onto Highway 70 and was going around the curve. I realized that the cars were traveling so fast that they were not able to see my car in time to slow down. I pulled over until the traffic cleared and a very kind gentleman pulled behind me. He got out to ask me if I needed help. I explained my situation and he obviously saw I had my sons with me so he told me he would drive behind me to give me enough distance between the traffic to safely get me to the next service station. When we made it there, he went the extra mile and offered to take me and my sons all the way home. I accepted his gracious offer and left the car there until it could be taken to be repaired. Looking back, I see how dangerous that could have been but thank God, it wasn't. I am sure this stranger must have been our guardian angel sent straight from God. I had a great sigh of relief when we arrived safely home. I honestly don't even remember his name, but I will never forget his kindness and the time he took to help this damsel-in-distress. I truly pray that God blessed him for his concern and the action that he took as a result.

> *"Do not forget to entertain or show love to strangers, for some have entertained angels without knowing it" Hebrews 13:2*

I pray also that you will take time to notice others in distress and reach out to them with God's love and the provisions He has blessed you with. We will never fully know what others are going through or the impact our kindness will have upon them and their children.

THE WINNOWING FORK

The year 2020 was quite a year! COVID, riots, a tumultuous election year, Lucifer rallies set up to worship Satan in twelve cities around our nation, BUT GOD! I am so thankful for the reminder that God is still on His throne!! He is not, nor never will be wringing His hands in the midst of our world's chaos. I do believe that God is awakening His church, the bride of Christ. He is allowing these distressing situations and is using this time to arouse sleepy Christians to rise up to worship, confess, pray, witness and marvel at the awesomeness of Jesus Christ and deepen their walk with Him. May it continue because every day there are more and more signs and evidence all around pointing to the soon return of Jesus Christ.

During one of my quiet times with the Lord, my attention was drawn to Jesus' words in Matthew 3:12 which says,

> *"His winnowing fork is in His hand and He will thoroughly clear His threshing floor and He will gather His wheat into the barn, but He will burn up the chaff with unquenchable fire."*

King David compared the wicked with chaff in Psalms 1:4-6 which states,

> *The wicked are not so, but they are like chaff which the wind drives away. For the LORD knows the way of the righteous, but the way of the wicked will perish.*

When I read about the wheat being gathered into the barn, but the chaff getting ready for unquenchable fire, I believe this is a powerful word picture about those who truly know Jesus versus those who profess to know him without evidence of a changed life or those that boldly reject Him.

I wonder why at funerals it is often stated that the deceased is in Heaven, yet during the life of that person, they had no time or place for God. They didn't want to be around God's people or do things to try to please God, but yet then when they die, people say they went to Heaven. I just wonder, why would someone want to spend eternity with someone they don't like or want anything to do with? Definitely something to ponder on. Eternity is too long to be wrong.

I would like to challenge you if you have doubts about if there even is a God, ask Him some questions. Ask Him if He is real and then listen to His response. Ask Him what you need to know about situations you have in your life and wait for His response. Then ask Him what He wants you to do about those situations. Wait until He responds and then obey His instructions. You will be amazed at what happens.

Oh, may we be diligent to represent Jesus well and share Him with others and the great love He has for everyone. The time is now. The hour is late! There is no time to delay! Jesus is coming back soon and only those that have a personal relationship with Jesus will go to Heaven. It is not enough to believe in God with your head, you must rather believe God in your heart and obey His word. May we be faithful until the Lord comes to take us home. Thank you, Jesus, for your amazing free gift of salvation for anyone who chooses to accept the best gift ever!

W.A.Y.

When I was in fourth grade, my family began attending Bethel Baptist Church in Ravenna, Ohio. They had a program for my age group called Willing Active Youth led by Mrs. Tucker. It was there that I met some new friends, Kim, Pam and Melissa and we had a great time learning and having fun together.

Now I am very goal-oriented, so I enjoyed the class very much because we were presented with lots of incentives for memorization challenges which sent me into action. I Corinthians 13, the love chapter, was chosen to memorize so I immediately began working on that so I would win the prize.

When the day came to recite what we had learned, I was prepared and ready and I won my first album by Evie Tornquist. I played it as soon as I got home and was so happy with my accomplishment. I did not just play it once but over and over and the lyrics became embedded into my mind and heart.

As I ponder this memory, I can see how God was using the church, youth programs, teachers and positive role models in my life to impart God's truth, which is still impacting me to this day. I am so grateful that my parents were intentional in exposing me to positive role models and Christian environments which have been very influential in my life.

This is a warning and reminder to me that others are observing and learning from my life, so I want to make sure it is a positive influence.

I believe that one day when God makes us aware of how our lives have positively touched others, I am confident we will be very thankful that we took the time to invest in others and planting seeds of God's truth in their lives.

I am sure when Mrs. Lucille Tucker met Jesus, He welcomed her and said,

> *"Well done, though good and faithful servant, come on in!"*
> *Matthew 25:23*

PS. I can still quote I Corinthians 13 with a touch of review! :)

WE ARE JUST "GOD" CONTAINERS

Have you ever met people that are just so inspiring that you will never forget the life lessons that they exemplified? Well, I am privileged to know two different ladies that have greatly impacted my life.

The first lady's name was Judy. We attended our church together and she was a dear friend of our family. I was only a teenager, but I can still remember where we were when we received the call that she had had a massive stroke. She was only thirty years old, and she became paralyzed on one side. Although this presented big challenges in the aftermath of that, she was a very determined woman and God strengthened her for her journey.

As she was recovering, she created a scrapbook of her life to help her remember and she used it as a testimony to God's grace. I remember when she shared it with me, she always reminded me that her body was just the container, but God was the one within her helping her to do so many things and shine for Him. She learned to cook one-handed and was always making yummy treats to share with others. She also began a card ministry to encourage others. When I was in college, I would frequently receive a card from her to let me know that she was praying for me every day. She would also visit nursing homes to encourage the residents as well. She did not have an easy life and had many challenges, but she had a smile and she gave praise to Jesus for how God helps her, always in the present tense form. She is now with Jesus, but I will be forever grateful for her influence in my life.

Another lady who has also had tremendous influence on my life as an adult is my dear friend, Angeline. The minute we met, our hearts were connected when she shared how she desired God to use her to help mentor young people but wasn't sure about how since she was in a wheelchair. She, too, had had a stroke and was paralyzed on one side. At that time, the REACH Mentoring Ministry was just beginning, but I gave her the opportunity to partner with us. God has truly used her in so many lives since that day, including my own.

We reach out to foster and at-risk young people and those that have aged out of the foster care system. They all love Angeline and she is able to relate to them on so many levels. I love it when they try to give excuses, but Angeline responds with, "No buts!"

She continues to shine, show up and share with everyone that she comes in contact with, and she just doesn't let things stop her. One time in our mentoring club, she was asked the question, "How does it feel to be handicapped?" She immediately responded, "I'm not handicapped, I just have limited mobility!" We were all speechless at her immediate response.

I am incredibly thankful for the privilege to call her my dear friend. We joke that we are each other's person because we are so connected by heart and we share the same Heavenly Father.

So, just remember, we are all just God containers and He uses every single one of us to point others to Him. Don't ever make excuses, but trust God to enable you to fulfill His purpose for your life.

2 Corinthians 4:7 says it best,

> *"But we have this treasure in jars of clay to show that this all-surpassing power is from God and not from us."*

WHAT'S THE CHANCE?

I attended two different Christmas parties where I experienced two surprising miracles. This reminded me how much that God not only loves me and knows what I need, but He loves to delight me.

The first dinner party happened many years ago. We had numbers on our name tags which matched up with the door prizes, however there were not prizes for everyone. Well, I noticed a DVD player with a big red bow on it. Now, I only had a VHS tape player, so I got excited about the possibility of winning that gift. I said a little prayer about winning that, but I know God does not always answer yes to our requests. The Bible does say though, "We have not because we ask not", so I prayed. Then when they announced the winners—my name and number was called and not just any gift, but the one with the big red bow. I was beyond excited and just amazed at God's goodness!

The most recent Christmas party demonstrated again just how much God knows me and loves me. I was playing a game, and I was waiting for my birthdate to be called, but I was one of the last players to be called. So, when my birthdate was finally called, I went to the board which had covered solo cups attached. I selected one, pulled out a slip of paper which had a number to be matched with one of the gifts on the table. The gifts were unwrapped and the majority of them were wine bottles which I did not want since I do not drink. There was only one soft blanket up there. Now anyone that truly knows me, they would be certain that would be my pick, not that I needed another blanket, but I would be delighted to share it with one of our foster youths. Well, my number was one and when I walked to the table with the gifts, lo and behold, the number on the blanket was one! Just absolutely amazing! As I returned to my seat, my smiles abounded and my heart was filled with overflowing gratitude for God's kindness to me and giving me exactly what He knew I would desire because He knows me so intimately.

Matthew 10:26-31 talks about how much value God places on us and verse 30 says,

> *"Even the very hairs of your head are all numbered."*

Now, I know this is a full-time job, because my hair falls out constantly. Psalms 139 also records how God created me and there is not one detail that escapes His attention about my life. I am beyond grateful for the amazing loving care He continues to demonstrate toward me.

These blessings definitely did not happen by chance, but a very intentional God has intentionally chosen me to be His beloved daughter, and He loves to delight me!

WHEN I AM AFRAID

I have been around for many years now and only in the last five years of my life have I learned just how powerful FEAR actually is. It controls most every single human, but our reactions differ from extreme to very moderate responses.

What really made me aware of this concept is COVID 19. The fear of getting sick and dying kept us from our families, loved ones, work, pleasurable activities, church, even just talking with our friends and acquaintances in person. We hid our faces with masks and isolated ourselves in our homes with very little socialization for months to even years. As we all remember, the entire world shut down for a season, and now our world is experiencing the consequences of this.

What I have learned from all this is that when I trust God, though I will still experience fear, I don't have to allow it to paralyze and control me.

I have a Father who loves me and who remains large and in charge. He is Sovereign over all, and His name is Jesus. I remind myself that if He can create and sustain this world, keep the stars in place, keep us the perfect distance from the sun, hold the ocean back, provide food and water through the ages and everything else we need for existence, I need not worry when things seem scary and out of control.

As a nurse, I like to ponder about how God made our amazing bodies function without any help from us. This is very evident in our reproductive system, hearts beating 60-100 times per minute, our liver and kidneys filtering and eliminating toxins, our digestion system processing food and drink, our lungs oxygenating our bodies, etc.

These are just a drop in the bucket of all the body systems that are continuously working around the clock to keep us alive and healthy.

I actually am thankful for that distressful season we endured, for God has used this in my life to embolden me to encourage others and share God's love with others. I am also much more intentional in teaching my granddaughter truths that will help support and give her a foundation of faith for the rest of her life.

One of the ways I have done this is to share the old Steve Green scripture video for kids that I had also used for my own sons. The one that has been helpful to her is the scripture song lyrics that say, "When I am afraid, I will trust in You, God."

Recently, my heart was so touched when my son caught her on her monitor while she was in her bed singing, "When I am afraid, I will trust You, God." She continued to sing it over and over to herself. I believe God heard her little voice and was smiling and comforting her when no one else was around. This is a powerful lesson that I pray she will never forget as long as she lives.

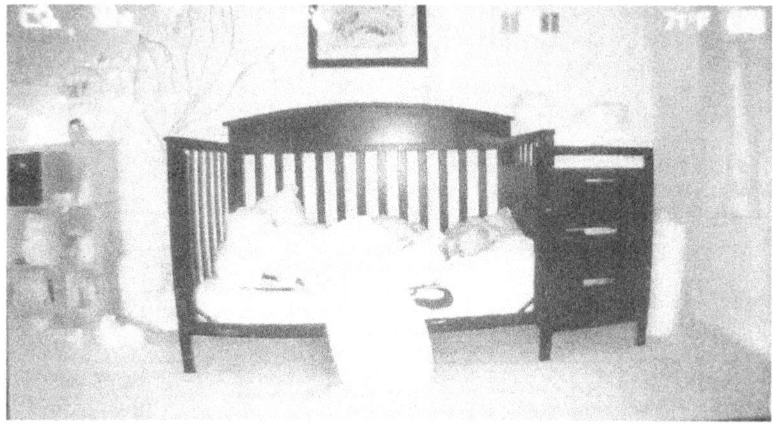

John 16:33 says,

> *"I have told you these things, so that in me you may have peace. In this world you will have trouble. But take heart! I have overcome the world."*

This is how I maintain my confidence!

I hope you will do the same along with our sweet Abigail!

WHO'S ON YOUR HITLIST???

Kind of an unusual title for a devotion, so let me explain.

My sister, Cathy is two and a half years older than me, and she has a totally different personality than me. I have always looked up to her and I still love being around her when we have the opportunity. She is fun, outgoing, vivacious and she always has lots of friends that love to be around her as well. When we get together, our times include lots of laughing, reminiscing and playing games together. By the way, she is very competitive! She likes to cook yummy food to bring back memories for me, and I am so incredibly thankful for her. She knows Jesus and has been very bold in her witness especially after she accepted Christ. She has always been gifted with gab and has been able to communicate God's love very effectively. One of her friends even said one time that she would actually be willing to pay money to spend more time with Cathy. Wow!

She is very independent and got her first job at A&W Root Beer stand when she was just fifteen years old and prior to that she did a lot of babysitting. I followed in her footsteps and so we worked together for several years at A&W. At eighteen years old, she decided to move out of our home and move in with a girlfriend to have her own place. It was definitely a sad day for me. I felt like I was losing her, but thankfully she welcomed me to hang out with her often at her apartment, which I loved doing.

Though we had been raised to serve God and attend church, she allowed this to fall aside in her life during this season. However, God is faithful to draw us back to Himself, and after some time, Cathy came back to the Lord, and she became passionate to share

God's amazing love with her friends that did not have a relationship with Jesus.

She made a list of all her friends at that time and labeled that her "hitlist," which meant she wanted them to come to Jesus as she had. I don't remember how many exactly were on her list, but I believe that most of them have turned to Jesus and have continued to faithfully serve Him through the years. I am so proud of her for this, and I am confident God is also smiling over her.

So, the challenge is… who are we praying for in our lives to come to know and experience the love of Jesus? Jesus' final command before He returned to Heaven was to go and preach the gospel to everyone, everywhere. Now, preaching does not need to be obnoxious, but when we become a caring friend and just live out God's love and His light within us, it will draw others to HIM! So, let's be more intentional to shine and share with our own "hitlist" of friends.

> *"Go into all the world and preach the gospel to all creation." Mark 16:15*

WITHOUT ASKING

School had always been easy for me and I had always been a straight A student, so when I was accepted into nursing school, I expected it to be the same. I was eager to do my best and work hard and was confident I would do well. But I can tell you this from experience, nursing school was very different. It was by far one of the most confusing and stressful environments. I studied the hardest I ever had and was happy when I received at least a passing grade. I quickly understood the meaning of the slogan, "C's equal degrees."

As we were nearing graduation, our class was diligently looking to locate a job, but not me. To be honest, I was already so stressed out with finishing that the thought of searching for a job overwhelmed me even more, plus I had no idea where to begin.

Well, I love to walk and I used that time to try to relax and decompress. One day I went outside to walk around the pond and prayed for help. I asked God for guidance and direction to the job He had for me. I was so new, I didn't know what type of job I would be good at, but I was sure He did. I prayed specifically that someone would offer me a job and I would not even have to ask for it. Sure enough, the next day when I had clinicals, my supervisor called me into her office. She reminded me that she had offered me a job earlier and the offer was still available if I was interested. I am not sure, but I imagine my jaw dropped at the speed in which God responded to my prayer.

I accepted her offer on the spot in her office, because I was confident God had answered my prayer by providing the perfect job for me at the time without me even having to ask.

"Your Father knows what you need before you ask Him." Matthew 6:8

"We have not because we ask not." James 4:1-3

I still marvel at how God has continually met my needs and actually has done more for me than I could have ever imagined.

So next time, you are wondering which way to go or what is best, trying praying and asking God for help and guidance. Trust His promise in *Malachi 3:10 which says,*

"Test me in this, says the Lord Almighty, and see if I will not throw open the windows of Heaven for you and I will pour out more blessings than you have room for."

YOU CAN DO IT!!

When I was in nursing school, God sent me three different families that believed in me, encouraged me and supported me with scholarships through that season of my life. I am so incredibly thankful for their encouragement, prayers and support because they helped give me the ability to succeed. These families were the Stancil's, Lamms and the Helms. All of them have now graduated to be with Jesus, but their legacy and influence lives on in my heart.

I first met Carl and Margie Lamm at a Rotary club meeting when I was awarded a scholarship that they had provided. After that initial meeting, they loved and supported me, and I actually felt like part of their family. Even up until he went to Heaven, over twenty-one years later, Carl would call me on Fridays to remind me to pray for our country and he always thanked me for all I am now doing for our community.

I made occasional visits to see him and would take him some type of sweet treat. I treasured this relationship and considered it a privilege to be his friend. I miss him a lot.

I met the Stancil family at a church singing. Afterwards, Betsy complimented me on my sons and asked me about my family. I let her know I was a single mom and was currently in nursing school at JCC. She immediately responded that they provided scholarships for students there. She also asked me for my address, because she said she wanted to send me some gas coupons. I was surprised at this amazing kindness and asked what her name was, but she responded, "It doesn't matter." I had no idea who this kind woman was, until a gentleman came up and said, "Hello, Betsy Stancil."

True to her word, later that very week, I received gas coupons and this happened periodically the rest of my school days. Just amazing. I enjoyed a long-term relationship with this family and also felt included as part of their family for many years.

Later that week, I was called to the financial office at JCC to inform me that Mr. Mokie Stancil had come in on Monday and was trying to get a scholarship for me, but the funds were already distributed.

A little later, I was asked to speak to the donor appreciation dinner from the scholarship I had received from the prior year. I was happy to do so, although it was my first time speaking to this large group of benefactors. I knew I could not refuse to say thank you for all of God's blessings on my life and the people that He had used to help me along the way.

The week after I spoke, I received a card from the Helms family. They told me they had heard me speak at the banquet, and also that Mokie Stancil had been speaking to them on my behalf. The note proceeded to let me know that it gave them great pleasure to help support me and included a very generous check to help me in school and for my family. This also began another long-term friendship, and I enjoyed visiting them occasionally and taking them goodies to just let them know how much I appreciated their investment in our lives.

When I met Mrs. Dot Helms, she told me she also had been a nurse and understood the stress school was. She had a very special way she spoke and always told me, "*You can do this, Susan!*" I have never forgotten her words of encouragement and shared this with my sons and many other people.

As I reflect back on that season of my life, I have no idea how I would have made it through, had I not had all these angels placed in my life to help me soar over all the hurdles that were so challenging. I truly thank God for placing them there at just the right time to help me finish the race I was running.

> *Therefore, since we are surrounded by such a great cloud of witnesses, let us throw off everything that hinders and the sin that so easily entangles, and let us run the race marked out for us. Hebrews 12:1-2*

Now that all three couples are with Jesus, I bet they are all still cheering me and their other loved ones to finish the race even more so now.

They were such wonderful, amazing role models to my life and I pray that I will be able to follow their example by investing and blessing others just like they did.

PS. I wonder if they might have started an amen corner in Heaven?

YOUR GOD STORY

Now that you have read some of my God stories, it is time to begin recording your own. May God bless you as you remember and record all His faithfulness, love, provision, and redemption in your own personal life. If you can't think of anything, just ask Him to remind you all the ways He has worked in your life and I'm confident He will answer your request. He loves you so much. and I can't wait for you to begin to recall your account of His lavish love in your life. If you would like to share any of your stories with me, you can email me at susan.stem64@gmail.com. I would love to hear from you.

ACKNOWLEDGEMENTS

I first want to thank everyone that has bought the first volume of my book and has encouraged me to keep writing! It has been so honoring to hear from many of you that my God stories have encouraged and inspired you. I honestly believe that this is why God put the desire in my heart long ago. Some of you even shared that you would also like to write a book yourselves and I hope that you will do just that. I hope that with this next volume many more lives will be blessed and given hope.

I am so grateful for Ruth Griffin who has once again done an excellent job editing and the publishing of this second volume. She has been so encouraging to me to continue to write.

Jim Brown, once again you have done an outstanding job with the cover illustration. I appreciate your willingness to work with me again on this project. Your talent is incredible.

Finally, I want to give all the praise to God for allowing me this amazing journey and now enabling me to share how He has transformed my trials and testing into a testimony for others to be encouraged. I will continue to pray that He uses these words to bring many others into a love relationship with HIM and that He receives all the glory and praise.

ABOUT THE AUTHOR

Susan grew up in Ohio in a loving, Christian family where she learned to love Jesus. She has always had a heart to minister to those that are unloved and outcasts and God gave her a dream to have a camp one day where young people would be loved and nurtured. This led her to attend Word of Life Bible Institute where she was able to learn God's word and put it into practice by serving in the youth camps. Upon graduation, she ministered with Youth for Christ in the detention centers and served as a houseparent for the Christian Life Home for pregnant unwed girls. She has two sons which she began homeschooling until she began to go to nursing school in 2003. She graduated in 2007 and then became a foster mom in 2011 after her sons graduated and went off to Word of Life Bible Institute. She volunteered at Royal Family Kids Camp for foster youth as their nurse in 2015 and continued as a volunteer with Teenworks mentoring program. In 2016, God led her to be the Founder and Director of the REACH Mentoring Ministry for foster and at-risk young people, where she has coordinated and led events at children's homes, began mentoring clubs in the public schools, and directed summer day camps since 2021. She is currently working as a school nurse which she absolutely loves and provides her ministry opportunities every day. She is continually striving to be a conduit of love to everyone she encounters.

Susan has been happily married to Jay Stem for the past six and a half years. God has blessed her with two wonderful sons, Benjamin, John-Mark and his wife, Anna and their two daughters, Abigail and Elaine. She loves being Grams, which brings her such joy and delight and is grateful for each and every opportunity she gets to spend with them.

She also loves to read, write, participate and lead Bible studies, and serve at her church. She loves to spend time with her family and friends and be adventurous and check things off on her bucket list.

Most of all, Susan loves Jesus and she is continually amazed how God is continuing to redeem her life and provide so many opportunities to share her testimony with others.

www.ingramcontent.com/pod-product-compliance
Lightning Source LLC
Chambersburg PA
CBHW061737050726
47598CB00002B/510

* 9 7 8 1 9 5 4 8 1 8 6 2 0 *